C000270500

Colin writes as he lives – wit
which is seldom seen. The top
the manner in which he does ᵢ
have not seen it that way before.

These things all make this book well worth a few hours
of your time, as well as the time of your friends and family.
Take your time and enjoy with Colin Murray in *Life Matters
– Confronting the Challenges of our Times*.

You are in safe hands.

Craig Denham
Lead Pastor – Love Church, Glasgow and Paisley

Colin Murray's writing is a fine example of pastoral
encouragement for God's people. These devotions without
doubt encourage the discouraged, give hope to those feeling
a sense of hopelessness and leads the reader closer to Jesus
Christ.

Gavin Hunter
Pastor of Stoneleigh Baptist Church

Colin has produced a collection of writing that is bold in the
range of topics covered, yet at the same time deeply personal.

I first met Colin when I was pastoring a Church in
Stirling and then got to know him well when I was pastoring
a Church in the North of Scotland. Like the author himself,
this book is sincere, honest, and wise. The engaging writing
style and Colin's trademark wit help us to connect with the
wisdom herein.

Colin describes his faith with vulnerable authenticity. In
so doing, he allows us a powerful glimpse of the God he sees
as the constant strength and hope of his life.If you are ready to

be challenged, encouraged, and moved, I highly recommend that you read this book.

Gordon MacKintosh

I am delighted to have the opportunity to commend to you Pastor Colin Murray's excellent book, "Life Matters". You will find, in the multitude of subjects dealt with in these pages, reason to return and dip into this book time and again over the years. Its well written and crafted words will help you find encouragement from Jesus Christ appropriate to the happenings and thoughts that are part of being human.

These words would have carried heavenly anointing whenever they had been penned. The fact that the book is published in the process of Colin living with MND, undoubtedly gives them an extra authority. As this book is read, my prayer is that it will be used to bring real help from a real God into real need.

Knowing Colin's heart for God and people, I think he would rejoice with thankfulness to hear of such fruit from his labours.

Rev. Kenny Borthwick
Teaching Pastor Martin's Memorial Church Stornoway
And former leader of C.L.A.N Gathering

LIFE
MATTERS

CONFRONTING THE CHALLENGES OF OUR TIME

COLIN MURRAY

Troubador Publishing Ltd
Unit E2 Airfield Business Park
Harrison Road, Market Harborough
Leicestershire LE16 7UL
Tel: 0116 279 2299
Email: books@troubador.co.uk
Web: www.troubador.co.uk

ISBN 978-1-80514-123-5

British Library Cataloguing in Publication Data.
A catalogue record for this book is available from the British Library.

Printed and bound in the UK by TJ Books Limited, Padstow, Cornwall
Typeset in 11pt Minion Pro by Troubador Publishing Ltd, Leicester, UK

Matador is an imprint of Troubador Publishing Ltd

Contents

Contents

Contents

Foreword

John Merson

When I was a kid in Portsoy, I was more into fishing than football but occasionally I would head up to the playing fields for a kick around. It was there that I would encounter "Duracell", the one with the copper top! That was one of several nicknames Colin had, back in the day, because of his fiery red hair. For a spell, he used to call me "Immersion Heater".

In our youth, we played the odd game of football, but we were never particularly close. Over time the "Battery" and "Heater" went their separate ways. Twenty years later, however, Colin landed up buying a house in Schoolhendry Street, and the newly acquired property happened to be directly opposite the Merson family home.

Over the next 15 years, Colin got to know my folks and had regular conversations with them. One day Colin announced to my father that after 40 years as an agnostic he had become a follower of Jesus. My father was genuinely thrilled to think that the painter across the street had come to a living faith. This news was relayed to me in Aberdeen. As a result, the Battery and the Heater landed up having a fresh encounter. The Battery evidencing new life and power, the Immersion Heater bubbling up with excitement at Colin's new-found faith.

Since then, Colin has become a precious brother and has impressed me greatly with his undaunting commitment to realise two things: Firstly, to plant a Church in Portsoy, which is no small challenge, and secondly, to keep sharing his faith with others, particularly through the vehicle of writing. Over the years, Colin has fine-tuned his writing skills, becoming an accessible communicator to the wider populace.

In his latest book *"Life Matters"*, Colin explores a range of topics centred on the best and worst of human nature with much clarity and a rare honesty. Topics range from life-controlling behaviour to freedom in the Spirit. From human loss and rejection to hope and acceptance. From envy and insecurity to grace and confidence. From anguish and despair to true joy and hope. It's all there! In an age of meaningless sound bites and media saturation *"Life Matters"* will give you something to richly chew on but not enough to choke on.

Like many others, I was deeply disappointment to hear the news that Colin had been diagnosed with MND, a wretched muscle wasting condition that offers no remission or medical cure. Since being diagnosed, Colin has chosen to be open and public with his MND battle. Midst the daily challenges, Colin continues to fight the good fight of faith. His faith remains the bedrock of his existence, giving him hope and perseverance midst the daily struggles and helping him to maintain an eternal perspective.

As the disease takes greater hold of his body, the Duracell Lad only knows too well that his battery power is becoming increasingly flat. However, through his writings and blogs, Colin remains steadfast in the belief that God's power is made perfect in his weakness. Though outwardly wasting away, he can testify to being recharged daily though the Spirit. All this comes through authentically in his writings.

In *"Life Matters"* Colin insists that despite being part of a broken and suffering humanity, we are all deeply valued by God. If we were ever in doubt with regards to our true value in the cosmos then Christ's twisted and tortured body, spreadeagled on the cross in an agonising posture of self-giving love for a lost world, should utterly dispel all our fears. For the cross proclaims an undeniable truth: God will not be God without humanity.

The cross says emphatically and unequivocally that we matter. You matter, faith matters, forgiveness matters, renewal matters, struggle matters, suffering matters, grace matters, acceptance matters – indeed, Life Matters!

All these topics, and many others, are thoughtfully touched upon in *"Life Matters"*. I trust that, like me, you will find the book an honest, relatable, and encouraging read, as Colin seeks to bring spiritual truth and wisdom to bear on all of life.

Enjoy!

ACKNOWLEDGEMENTS

A published book would never be possible, particularly so quickly, without a small team of precious friends who are selfless in their support and expertise.

Paulina Honig, as in 2010 with my first book Papering over the Cracks, responded lovingly to my SOS call at short notice to help me with proofreading and formatting. Paulina's support and meticulous editing has once more been invaluable.

I am so grateful to John Merson for writing such a humbling and heartfelt foreword. John and I do go back many years to our Immersion Heater and Carrot Heid Battery days in Portsoy! He has been a wonderful blessing in my life with wise spiritual counsel and Godly example during my highest highs and lowest lows of ministry – a true friend and brother.

There are so many people I want to thank on my spiritual journey, too many to mention. I value so much their mentorship, their guidance, their correction, and their encouragement.

And I would also like to thank those precious friends who encouraged me to put a varied selection of the blogs, devotionals, and articles I have written over the years into a published work.

Lastly, and most importantly, thanks be to my Lord and Saviour for His grace and faithfulness through many trials of my life. From the early days of my MND diagnosis I knew He had a greater plan and purpose for my life. And I am thankful for what He is doing through my withering body but unbreakable spirit.

Great is thy faithfulness.

Our Example, Not Our Faith, Is What Defines Us

Human behaviour is very difficult to understand, even at the best of times. After all, we are all complex beings and our behaviour is often a defence, a way of concealing true motives and thoughts and our true selves. To be brutally honest, 1 can cringingly look back on numerous occasions in the last 20 years when my behaviour has been anything but Christlike.

From experience, I have noticed that relationships of any-kind seldom seem to die a natural death. They tend to be assassinated by pride, greed, lust, complacency, mistrust, betrayal or simply misunderstanding.

A casual google search will reveal many seemingly great men and women of faith in business. politics, entertainment, or sport, who fell spectacularly from grace because their behaviour did not match up with their reputation. Most bad behaviour is rooted in fear and insecurity which tends to manifest in controlling, deceitful and reckless behaviour.

I sometimes hear that religious or "churchy" folk think they are better than everybody else! It's probably something that I would have willingly agreed with for many years without having any real evidence to back it up. But I don't honestly believe there is much credence in such sweeping statements. There is no doubt there are arrogant or haughty Christians, but from my experience I have found the many I have encountered to be humble and unassuming with a willingness to grow spiritually and serve others.

True Christianity is not an exercise in simply being good, looking good or smelling good. It is more about being willing to change – to grow in love, grace, and humility, not simply in knowledge, status, or performance.

Every one of us, regardless of what we believe or who we follow, can make mistakes, and get things wrong. The boundary that separates the well-intended from the well-behaved; the great gulf between words and deeds can be crossed in all our lives.

We've all acted in ways that made us ashamed or at least greatly embarrassed later – in other words: we all have the capacity to goof up! Hypocrisy, that almost-universal human trait, afflicts just about everyone. It's easy to believe in a high, noble cause or principle, but quite a bit harder to always follow it or live by it.

Genuine faith goes far beyond any sermon or prayer session or ritual or set of dos and don'ts. Instead, it challenges us to truly change, to alter what we do, so that our behaviour is more Christ-like than self-like or idol-like.

THE POWER OF GRACE – CHRISTIANITY'S GREAT DISTINCTIVE

In 1987, an IRA bomb buried Gordon Wilson and his twenty-year-old daughter Marie beneath five feet of rubble. Gordon alone survived and, unbelievably, he instantly forgave. He said of the callous bombers, "I have lost my daughter, but I bear no grudge. I shall pray, tonight and every night, that God will forgive them". His words did more than tickle the secular media's ears and out of one man's grief, the world got a glimpse of grace – not shallow grace or hyper grace but simply God's undeserved and unmerited grace. The power of Grace is also incredibly difficult to get our heads round because it goes against the grain of all human feelings and reactions, and our carnal minds are naturally more attuned to justice and revenge.

Grace is, or at least should be, Christianity's great distinctive over every other religion, worldview, or ideology. It's the one thing the world cannot replicate, and the one thing it craves above all else, for only grace can bring hope and transformation to a jaded and often embittered perilous world.

Grace will always triumph over revenge because it has no conditions attached to it.

When we have been truly touched by God's grace, when we are really in the grip of grace, we will no longer look on those who go off the rails as "those bad or evil people" or "those poor people who need our help." We see everyone as equal value. No abject failures or born losers. No in-crowd or out-crowd, nor must we search for signs that someone is worthy of our love.

Grace teaches us that God loves because of who God is, not because of who we are.

Let's Not Live With Regret

Regrets? I think everyone has regrets, and people who say they haven't are either liars or narcissists!

Regret for the time we lost our temper.

Regret for the day we lost control.

Regret for that decision we made that backfired spectacularly.

Regret for the years we lost when we neglected our priorities.

Regret for that wrong relationship that ended acrimoniously.

Regret for getting into that relationship in the first place!

I sometimes see stones piled up on beaches and they remind me of how we pile up our regrets: one guilty stone piled up on top of another. We add these regrets to our load one at a time. They get heavy to carry. We get tired and weary. How can we have dreams and hope for the future when all our energy is spent looking back through the rear-view mirror of life?

To be honest, I have spent too much of my life living with regrets, beating myself up and obsessing about things I have done and said that I know only too well I cannot change. But the Apostle Paul reminds us in Romans 8 Chapter 1 "There is no condemnation for those in Christ Jesus".

Where do we finally get relief and find solace? In the most comforting Bible verses: "Come to me, all of you who are tired and heavy laden, and I will give you rest. Accept my teachings and learn from me, because I am gentle and humble in spirit, and you will find rest for your lives. The teaching I ask you to accept is easy; the load I give you to carry is light". (Matt. 11:28—30).

Jesus says He is the solution for weariness of soul and unresolved regret. Regrets are simply wasted thoughts that eat into our time and dominate our life preventing us from truly living a joyful and fulfilling life. Can I encourage you this morning to go to Him with all that you carry in prayer?

Worship Dissolves Weariness

Are you struggling with weariness and lethargy just now? Many of us are, which is perfectly understandable after the Covid years with spells of lockdown. But even at the best of times, before we act and do something we are truly called to do, we often felt weary and lethargic with sometimes a sense of disillusionment. But when we are invigorated by a cause or a vision much greater than ourselves, we become energised again.

We often don't take the first steps towards our true calling in life because we fear the future will mirror our past, as we have been conditioned to believe that history will repeat itself. We reflect on our failures rather than focus on the possibilities of the future. But being willing and humble enough to grow spiritually allows transformation to blot out our past failures.

Fresh beginnings, offering hope, can give us a new lease of life if we neither denounce nor belittle. If instead we can soothe and console by reconstructing the broken pieces of yesterday, mending them and reinforcing them with boldness and courage like never before, that would be a beautiful and powerful thing.

Sometimes our weariness is not because we're active or busy. All too frequently it is because many of the things that we're running from are the very things we should be running to. The pressures of life will grind us into sand and pulverise us into particles – but only if we let them.

Worship dissolves weariness. There is no weariness in worship. When I personally feel tired and weary, I always find the best remedy in worship and in Scriptures, like this one in Isaiah that awaken me out of my slumber:

"He gives power to the faint, and to him who has no might he increases strength. Even youths shall faint and be weary, and young men shall fall exhausted; but they who wait for the Lord shall renew their strength; they shall mount up with wings like eagles; they shall run and not be weary; they shall walk and not faint". (Isaiah 40:29-31)

Gaslighting –
You Are Not Crazy
or Over-Sensitive

It's only in the last few years that "Gaslighting" has become a popular and much used buzzword in relation to spiritual and emotional abuse. Gaslighting is a form or emotional abuse that derives its name from the 1938 British theatre play *Gas Light*.

In this disturbing play, a guy called Jack Manningham terrorises his wife Bella by leading her to doubt her perception of reality. Bella, in turn, is comforted only by the one reality she can trust: The dimming gaslights that run parallel with Jack's early evening antics. As part of these manipulative antics, Jack hides household items then blames his wife for misplacing them, which plunges her into the depths of perplexity and self-doubt. Her only shred of sanity is the gaslight's flickering flame.

Anyone affected by the bite of narcissism of any kind does not feel it straight away, and they may even feel they deserve the criticism and abuse. The narcissist develops the uncanny ability to make others seem unstable, uncertain, confused, and insecure. Sadly, this behaviour occurs in a variety of scenarios, such as in the home, the workplace, and even the Church. In fact, we are allowing ourselves to be abused if we keep apologising when we haven't done anything wrong, just to keep the peace.

Perhaps the most frightening thing about the gaslighted or narcissist's bite is that it nearly always comes without leaving a physical wound. The trauma inflicted invariably rears its ugly head in the shape of humiliation, extreme mood swings, threats of retribution, character assassination, as well as isolation from family and friends.

Spiritual and emotional abuse have much in common, but spiritual abuse seems to have an even more sinister twist because power, position, Scripture, and in some cases legal threats, can be wielded as weapons of castigation and control. The chosen target feels just as perplexed, wounded, and confused as any victim of emotional abuse, but experiences it from a more authoritative source: A seemingly holy source.

Jesus was angered at the spiritually abusive tactics of the Pharisees. In Matthew 23, He expresses anger and lament through eight woes. He implies that the Pharisees put unfair expectations on other people that they themselves were unwilling adhere to. And that their lives were characterised by a grandiose sense of entitlement and inflated ego, rather than by humility and grace. Matthew 23 could have been written for today. Times may well change, but the tactics for emotional and spiritual abuse seem rehashed from generation to generation and from millennium to millennium.

There is someone out there who needs the hear the words, "You are not crazy, over-sensitive or imagining things". And now is a good time to shake off the shackles of control and gaslighting and to move into a new year with confidence, expectation, and renewed hope.

As Long As We Are Drawing Breath There Is Hope

For as long as we are drawing breath there is hope. It's often difficult to believe that when we are suffering deep emotional pain or seemingly terminal physical decline. No matter how many adversities life throws at us, our hope can never be extinguished unless we allow it to be. We can portray super confidence, super spirituality, or infallibility, yet harbour an element of self-doubt or insecurity.

Hope can certainly shrink and diminish but it can never disappear forever. From a small seed hope blossoms into a beautiful and exquisite flower that gives colour to our lives and to the lives of others. Hope doesn't mean solely focusing on all the positive aspects of life and ignoring or dismissing the negative ones.

Hope is the belief that beyond all darkness, suffering, and failure better days await us and that makes our journey and our struggles well worth it. Through taking time to reflect on our lives we will realise we have been in situations that have appeared hopeless and demoralising, but that we have overcome – somehow! Take confidence, strength, and encouragement from having overcome seemingly hopeless situations in the past and don't ever underestimate the power of human endurance and divine guidance. Genuine hope is not the super positivity we read about in self-help books. It is rooted in who we are and in the promises of our Maker.

A Smooth Sea Never Made
a Skilful Sailor

Unfortunately, the weather forecast can't predict the storms of our lives and so my MND diagnosis was the last thing I expected.

My mum's early death wasn't expected either, nor was my dad's suicide or any relationship breakups along the way.

Storms often come when everything seems calm and peaceful, and they have the capability to disorient us and throw us mercilessly from pillar to post. But once the storm is over, we will barely remember how we made it through; how we even managed to survive. We won't even be sure, whether the storm really is over.

But one thing is certain: When we stagger out of the storm, all battered, bruised and drookit, we won't be the same person who walked into it. We will be stronger, wiser, and more resilient. Let's go through the raging sea and lift ourselves up from the deck, and we will get back up stronger and more resolute than ever before.

Even a terminal diagnosis with imminent death is not the end. Jesus promises us: "And I give eternal life to them, and they will never perish; and no one will snatch them out of My hand". (John 10:28)

There's always a purpose for the storms of life. Where there are no storms there are no rainbows. The brightest rainbows are often after the toughest storms. When our storm is finally over, our prayers are answered. When the storm has passed, we've got a powerful testimony, wrapped up with a bow, ready to share with the world to comfort others.

Hope Creates Optimism and Disperses Despair

The key difference between hope and despair is the ability to believe in tomorrow. Most of the worthwhile achievements in this world have been accomplished by people who have kept persisting when all seemed lost without any hope at all.

Willpower, determination, and strength alone are commendable but will not help us to overcome whatever we're struggling with without faith. The key ingredient that makes everything else possible is hope. It's our hope for a better future that motivates us to make great sacrifices in the present.

We all hope for better health, less stress, loving relationships, and happy families, but when our prayers don't seem to get answered it's only natural for doubts and fears to creep in. Optimism is having the faith and conviction that leads to overcoming anything we are struggling with, ultimately leading to achievement. Nothing can be done without hope and confidence. Let's heed the words of the Apostle Paul: "We are afflicted in every way, but not crushed; perplexed, but not driven to despair". (2 Corinthians 4:8)

A Single Thread of Hope
Is a Powerful Thing

As I write this wee blog/devotional I am battling MND, a relatively rare neurological condition with no known cure. Over a third of sufferers die within a year of diagnosis, so hope of a supernatural healing, hope of a medical cure and the promise of eternal hope that we are promised in John 3:16 is what my life is anchored on.

Hope is that tiny seed or single thread inside of us that insists, despite all the evidence to the contrary, despite some horrendous past experiences, that something better awaits us if we have the courage to reach for it and to work for it and to fight for it. Practically anything is possible when we have hope. Even more is possible when we have faith, and still more is possible if we learn to love during the storm. Anything is possible if we are to embrace all three virtues.

The hope that God has provided for us is not merely wishful thinking, neither is it dependent on other people, possessions, or circumstances for its validity. Instead, biblical hope is an application of our faith that supplies a confident expectation in God's fulfilment of His promises.

The question is not, 'Will God keep his promises?' But: 'Will we build our lives upon them?' Too often we dismiss divine hope as religious nonsense or scoff at it as a crutch for the weak. But is our unbelief rooted in pride? If so, pride is the hidden reef that lurks menacingly within us that shipwrecks the soul.

Coupled with faith, grace and love, hope should be a huge part of the abiding characteristics in our lives. Never lose faith in yourself, and never lose hope; even a glimmer or a thread of hope is something to hold on to. Through times, when life throws its worst and then turns its back on us, there is always hope. "But I know, somehow, that only when it is dark enough can you see the stars" – Martin Luther King, Jr.

SELF-CONDEMNATION CAN RUIN YOUR LIFE

The defeatist and self-condemning mind says: 'My life is a failure – an absolute shambles'. So, we don't sleep well, and laughter, practically, becomes a thing of the past. It's as if disaster lurks around every corner. We expect failure – it's just a matter of time. The expectation of failure in our lives becomes a self-fulfilling prophesy. As a result, we're constantly anxious and fearing the worst, haunted by past decisions and experiences. Even when we witness clear green shoots of recovery, we obsess about what will probably go wrong.

Our world, in many ways, is crippled by anxiety. Jesus even warned us about this: "Be careful, or your hearts will be weighed down with the anxieties of life". (Luke 21:34 NIV).

We were created for far more than a life of self-condemnation and mind-numbing worry. We are never truly alone. Listen again to the simple and powerful words of that well-known hymn *What a friend we have in Jesus*.

One bad or soul-destroying chapter doesn't need to define our whole life. He has a new fresh chapter for our life and it's often near the end of a book that we read the best and most enthralling chapter.

LOYALTY IS FROM ABOVE, BETRAYAL FROM BELOW

I have heard it said that love often wears a mask to test loyalty. But defending a good friend in the middle of accusation and slander takes courage and shows real character. Often the best way to defend a friend is to speak up, but at other times the best support is to stay silent and refuse to jump on to the bandwagon or yield to the pressure of the opinions of others.

To my shame, I have allowed myself to be influenced by the plausibility of a one-sided story in the past, rather than listen to both sides, which clouded my ability to remain impartial.

Of course, we are not called upon to defend the indefensible: The crooked, the criminal, or the abuser, However, we are called upon to defend the friend who is being unfairly judged. If we master the discipline of being loyal to those who are not present, we build trust with those who are present.

True loyalty cannot be blueprinted, nor can it be produced on an assembly line. In fact, it cannot be manufactured at all, for its origin can only be the human heart – the centre of all self-respect and human dignity. It is a force that leaps into being only when conditions are exactly right for it, and it is a force very sensitive to betrayal. On the other hand, betrayal through gossip or slander never yet broke a chain of oppression or addiction, nor did it free a human soul. A true friend has seen the very best, as well as the very worst of us but loves and accepts us anyway.

Betrayal is mutiny. It's a violation of a trust and always an inside job. Troubles are part of life's package, and betrayal may well be included. Don't be surprised by betrayals. Don't always look for fairness here on earth – look instead where Jesus looked.

Jesus looked to the future: While surrounded by enemies He kept His mind on His Father. While abandoned on earth, He kept His heart on home. "In the future you will see the Son of Man seated at the right hand of Power and coming with the clouds of heaven". (Mark 14:62)

"My kingdom does not belong to this world," Jesus told Pilate. "My kingdom is from another place". In a nutshell: loyalty is from above; betrayal is from below.

By the way, The Father's loyalty to Jesus is the Father's loyalty to us. If ever we are betrayed, we'll have to remember that. When we witness the knives being sharpened or feel the imprint of a betrayer's kiss, remember His words: "I will never leave you; I will never abandon you".

SLANDER CAN CAUSE SERIOUS DAMAGE

Slander, at its most vicious, can cause serious damage. It can even destroy someone's marriage, ministry, business, family, as well as toy with a person's sanity.

The saying "Gossip dies when it hits a wise person's ears" is indeed true.

Our character and dignity can be mocked, abused, compromised, toyed with, ridiculed, or badmouthed, but it can never be taken away from us. We have the power to reset our boundaries, restore our confidence and dignity, to start afresh and rebuild what has been stripped from us.

Gossip typically centres on the negative aspects of someone's appearance, achievements, failures, or behaviour – never their success or good qualities. Some people gossip to seek revenge. When we dislike someone, or they get under our skin, there is often the temptation to seek out other people who share a mutual dislike for that person.

At the end of the day, gossip serves no purpose other than to hear ourselves spout and speculate about the misery of others. It's so easy to kick someone when they are down, but it's more gracious and honouring to either stay silent or offer support to the person in the firing line.

I cringingly recall a few years ago, when I was getting geared up to add my tuppence worth to a local scandal, being stopped in my tracks when I read these words:

"Great minds discuss ideas. Average minds discuss events. Small minds discuss people".

And don't we come under conviction when the person we were slagging off is vindicated or exonerated?

It is very difficult not to wade into speculative gossip and it's very easy to be caught off-guard when our heart has been slightly hardened. That's why I now firmly believe that, if at any time we feel like joining others in speaking words of slander about someone – don't speak the words! Instead, write what you want to say – write it in the sand near the water's edge!

In a culture saturated with conspiracy theories and gossip columns, where malicious claik is encouraged, it's no wonder we have become a nation of "Jessie Annies"!

The writer of Proverbs reminds us: "A perverse person stirs up conflict, and a gossip separates close friends".

Do Not Take Revenge, Dear Friends

If we really want to dislike someone, how about doing it alone? Let's face it, we have felt anger, injustice, and betrayal at some point in our lives and the temptation for revenge or reprisal would have been strong. However, recruiting a posse of supporters to help us fight our battles makes for an unlevel playing field.

In Leviticus, God reminded us that *He* is the Lord, not us. To hold a grudge and actively create our own judge and jury to determine that a person's wrong should not be forgiven is something no human being has the right or authority to do. Paul writes in Romans 12:19: "Do not take revenge, my dear friends, but leave room for God's wrath, for it is written: 'It is mine to avenge; I will repay,' says the Lord".

Let's focus on getting ahead, instead of even.

THERE IS NO TIMESCALE TO GRIEVE OR MOURN

Bereavement touches everyone, but no two people experience it in the same way. When someone we love dies, we are deeply saddened and we grieve their loss, regardless of our chosen faith or worldview. We are naturally sad for ourselves and for what we have lost – sad for the things we can no longer share. But we are also sad for the person who died and what they are missing; perhaps the blessing of grandchildren or sharing in our happiness and successes.

Losing someone we love is never easy, even if we believe they are with God in heaven. Our heart aches, and we miss them. We miss their presence, their laughter, their uniqueness, and their love. We even miss their quirkiness and frustrating habits!

If sadness and grieving are universal, the way we express them are uniquely personal. In the words of Scripture, "There is a time to mourn". (Ecclesiastes 3:4)

Life has its seasons of happiness and fulfilment, as well as the inevitable dark days, as we journey through life. There is no timescale with grief, and comments like: "He or she should be over it by now" or: "Stop feeling sorry for yourself – everyone deals with grief" are simply borne out of ignorance and judgementalism. Let us give words of comfort instead.

The blood of Jesus does cleanse and heal, but He is no cosmic magician who can obliterate all the pain and sadness in an instant, as some who follow Him seem to think. The way I grieve is not the same way as you grieve, but there is no right or wrong way to handle human loss.

The healing Lord is a God of compassion, and He ministers in an environment of truth and understanding. He grieves with those who grieve; He mourns with those who mourn.

You Are a Fighter – Look How Far You've Come!

Never forget how far you've come. All the times you've managed to push through when you felt you couldn't. All the mornings you dragged yourself out of bed, no matter how hard it was. All the times you wanted to give up but carried on regardless. Never forget how far you've come.

Those dark times, when you wanted to give up on life, yet you fought through another day. A fight is a fight. And life is often a battle, regardless of what the "name it and claim it", health and wealth preachers would have us believe.

No matter how many battles we have under our belt, it will continue to be a learning experience, and we can never prepare ourselves for every scenario. Awkward, harrowing, oppressive, shocking, numbing, and difficult situations will always present themselves, usually at the unlikeliest of times and from the unlikeliest of sources.

We'll just have to try and remain calm, work through the bad times and trust in a God who will never leave us or forsake us. Never forget the inner strength, character, and wisdom you've gained along the way. Thank God for your fortitude and your capacity to endure.

Even during the toughest times, we learn to "count our blessings, one by one".

Impartiality in a Dispute is the Essence of Grace

How often have we judged someone purely on the rumours we have heard about them or because of some nasty accusation with no credibility? To my shame, I certainly have, only to find out some time later, to my embarrassment, that the person concerned had been exonerated and therefore vindicated.

If we are honest, sometimes we do like to hear malicious gossip about someone, perhaps because we don't like them, are jealous of them or have a wee grudge against them that influences our ability to be impartial and want to see them "taken down a peg or two". Not, of course, because they deserve it, but because we think they need to be humbled when, in fact, we ourselves need to have more grace and understanding.

The other day, I was reminded of showing true wisdom and discernment regarding the Bible story of who the real mother of a baby boy was.

In the first book of Kings, Chapter 3, two mothers, who were living in the same house, each with an infant son, came to Solomon. One of the babies had died, and each mother claimed the remaining boy as her own. Calling for a sword, Solomon declared his judgment: The baby would be cut in two with each woman to receive half. One mother did not contest the ruling, declaring that if she could not have the baby then neither of them could. But the other begged Solomon: "Give the baby to her, just do not kill him!"

The king declared the second woman the true mother, as a mother would even give up her baby, if that was necessary, to save its life. We read later in the chapter: "All Israel heard of the judgment that the king had rendered, and they stood in awe of the king because they perceived the wisdom of God was in him to do justice". (1 Kings 3:28)

It is the Holy Spirit's job to gently convict but never condemn. God's job is to judge, and our job is to display grace and impartiality in any given situation or accusation, until we know the truth.

Naturally, we can get sucked in by plausibility or can be clouded by bias, resulting in digression from genuine discernment and wisdom. We may never know the whole truth, but it's tempting to grasp one side of a story and appoint ourselves judge and jury, ending up playing devil's advocate.

Showing impartiality is the essence of grace.

WE ALL HAVE THE RIGHT TO LIVE

In 2003, the New York Times magazine published an article by the late Harriet McBryde Johnson, a wheelchair bound quadriplegic and disabled-rights attorney. It highlighted her confrontation with Professor Peter Springer, a philosopher on Practical Ethics generally regarded as one of the most influential philosophers of our time. Johnson and Singer, both atheists, debated Singer's utilitarian philosophy advocating the killing of babies with serious disabilities.

Of course, we rightly question whether serial killers and those who commit heinous crimes should be allowed to live in the UK, but that's a debate for another day. I believe that no life should be cut short because of physical impairment. These poor souls are no burden to our country.

Describing herself as "a disability pariah", Johnson, who died in 2008, admitted her struggle for kinship, community, acceptance, and compassion. Representing the activist group *Not Dead Yet,* Johnston offered a humorous, persuasive, and emotional defence of her right to live. At one point she wondered, "Am I a person of faith after all?"

Having worked all my adult life, and now finding myself in need of assisted care and support due to my declining health, I wonder where I would fit into Peter Singer's utilitarian beliefs.

19th century German philosopher Fredrich Nietzsche resented Christianity for taking the side of all that is weak, base, and decrepit. According to him, religion based on pity went against evolution and its principles of fitness and competition. After all, Jesus of Nazareth was the first world leader to value those who had little value to the visible world – the pitiful, the social outcasts and the lame.

People like the late Harriet McBride Johnson, and many other physically impaired people, pose a challenging question: If we claim to be people of love and compassion, never mind faith, shouldn't we appreciate their right to exist as people made in God's image?

Can we, though, see the debilitated and impaired as God sees them? As God assured the prophet Samuel: "The Lord does not look at the outward appearance, but the Lord looks at the heart".

ONLY ALLOW KIND TENANTS IN YOUR HEAD

If we are being honest, we all let unwanted squatters and tenants reside in our napper from time to time! This only leads to stress and worry, with a massive dollop of obsessional negative thinking thrown in as well!

Let's ask ourselves: What is true and worthwhile in this and what is drama, false accusation or even something we need to genuinely apologise for?

It is wise, if not always easy, to let go of everything that's clearly drama, and take any accusation, whether merited or false, to the Lord in prayer. Each time that person invades your head space, confidently remind yourself that you have chosen not to play that game and, instead, focus on all that is good in your life add value and blessing to it.

Perhaps it's time to set clear boundaries for ourselves and for others, as well as accepting responsibility for the fact that who and what we allow to reside in our head will impact upon our quality of life – and that we always have a choice.

That choice is, to seek the presence of our true self; the essence of who we really are – unique and fearfully and wonderfully made. Then feel your heartbeat. It is a beautiful rhythmic beat that is uniquely yours. That heartbeat is the cadence to which our physical body and renewing mind marches.

It can be tempting, when we feel lonely, isolated, or vulnerable, to return to a relationship that has proved to be unhealthy and debilitating. But when we feel vulnerable and when fearful or obsessional thoughts try to seize control of our life, we can replace those thoughts with the truth of God's Word – "For God has not given us the spirit of fear; but of power, and of love, and of a sound mind". (2 Timothy 1:7)

The More We Pray,
the Less We'll Worry

I spent many years of my life as a constant worrier; I worried about anything, from finance to relationships, and if I didn't find something to worry about, that too would be a source of worry and stress! In a culture that promotes the myth of having it all together, I worried about practically everything – about not having enough work, about having too much work, about what others thought of me and even about what they didn't say about me.

I eventually came to realise that there's no greater enemy of joy and happiness than constant worry. I also realised that there's a subtle aspect to worry: If we care, we think we should worry. As if that will help somehow.

The reality is: Worry has absolutely no redemptive value. I have heard it said that worry is like a rocking chair: It gives us something to do but it doesn't get us anywhere!

Winston Churchill once remarked, "When I look back on all these worries, I remember the story of the old man who said on his deathbed that he had had a lot of trouble in his life, most of which had never happened".

Jesus said, "Can any one of you by worrying add a single hour to your life?" (Matthew 6:27)

The answer is: of course not! Worry, in the big scale of things, is irrelevant. We will never add one day to our life or one bit of precious life to our day by worrying. Worry, in a sense, is also irreverent, as it means distrusting God and His promise of "never leaving us or forsaking us".

The Apostle Paul urges us not to be anxious for nothing. How is that possible in a world of uncertainty, of illness, economic crisis, and strife? Instead of looking forward in fear, look upwards in faith and backwards in appreciation of past victories, as well as all we have overcome to reach this far. God's part is peace and protection. He enjoys perfect peace because he enjoys perfect power.

And He offers His peace to you to guard your heart.

Corrie Ten Boom once said, "Worry does not empty tomorrow of its sorrow, it empties today of its strength". And Paul writes in Philippians 4:6, "Do not be anxious about anything."

Worry is a killjoy; it specialises in worst-case scenario.

"Worry is the darkroom where negatives are developed". (Anon)

I have found that the more we pray, the less we'll panic. The more we worship, the less we'll worry. And the more patient we are, the less pressured we become. Sorrow looks back, worry looks around, but faith looks up.

So, look up today, friends, as His yoke is easy, and His burden is light.

WE ARE NEVER ALONE

Trying times often cause fear, worry, stress, and anxiety. As I write this, we are dealing with darkening nights, as well as increasing food and fuel bills which in turn can increase feelings of loneliness, isolation, and desperation. When we're lost in the dark caves of loneliness and isolation, it's easy to believe that we are alone and will always be alone; that we will always be straining our eyes looking for a glimmer of light.

Caves are mysterious, dark, and intimidating in their organic gloom. They seem to extend endlessly into some vast labyrinth. No wonder they are a setting for nightmares and horror films. But there's a deeper reason for the usefulness of the imagery: Caves can also function as vast echo chambers and, once trapped inside, the only voice we can hear clearly is our own.

For those of us battling loneliness and isolation, the thing that our minds crave more than anything – though, of course, I speak mainly for myself here – is companionship. We need friends who understand, who come alongside, who offer a hand up or an arm round the shoulder. Not fixers or analysts, not would-be therapists, not trite "name it and claim it" theologies – and certainly not those whose spiritual insecurities are such that they need other believers, especially pastors, to always be spiritually "sorted" or even flawless.

Even friends can't make us feel accepted all the time. Accomplishments will never truly make us feel secure, even though we crave that. Having lots of people around us doesn't mean we won't ever feel lonely. And sex, drink, gambling, spending money, eating chocolate, and fanatically watching sports – while deliciously distracting – are always temporary.

The truth is: We are never truly alone.

Yet, at times it can feel like we are stranded in isolation, reflecting on our bad experiences, sorrows, and failures and, no matter how much we try to see the light, everything seems bleak and hopeless.

If that applies to us, today, then maybe it's time to let God's love cover all things in our life. All secrets. All hurts. All hours of self-doubt. All minutes of constant worry.

Nowadays, technology makes it possible to have thousands of Facebook friends, yet we can still feel lonely, we can still feel emotionally and spiritually distanced in the unpredictability and weirdness of today's world.

But thanks to our gracious God we know that in Christ we are not, and never will be, spiritually distanced. The Lord Jesus is our best friend because He truly sticks closer than a brother (Proverbs 18:24).

Envy Only Leads to Loneliness and Isolation

I have heard it said that being jealous just shows how we really love or care about someone in relationships. But Jealousy is a caustic disease that eats away at our very soul. Genuine love, on the other hand, is a healthy, wholesome fruit of the spirit. This truth can be subtly mistaken to leave us with a distorted and immature view of relationships, where we can wrongly assume: The greater the love, the greater the jealousy. In fact, they are totally incompatible – one emotion leaves no room for the other. Jealousy would be far less torturous if only we understood that love is a passion entirely unrelated to our own and is divinely given.

Undoubtedly, we have all seen envy – real red-faced jealousy. Are we familiar with the scarlet forehead and the bulging veins of jealousy in relationships? What's the cure for jealousy? Trusting, and letting go of suspicion and accusation is the only cure. The root cause of jealousy, on the other hand, is always distrust.

In fact, envy is probably the most wicked of all human traits. It has been the potent mother of all broken relationships, tragedies, murders, and wars, since time began. Reprehensible though it is, jealousy is rather to be pitied than blamed. Its first victims are always those who harbour the feeling. Solomon reminds us: "Anger is cruel and destroys like a flood, but no one can put up with jealousy!" (Proverbs 27:4)

At the end of the day, envy is a symptom of being unaware or lacking appreciation of our own uniqueness and self-worth. Each of us has something to give that no one else has, but if we honestly believe we don't, we will always be jealous of what others have.

Envy can rear its ugly head in many ways: Our character, our relationships, our family, our accomplishments, our ministry, and our influence are often prime targets. There will always be someone willing to damage our reputation, put us down, gossip about us, belittle our accomplishments, and question our motives. It is a reality that we must face.

However, we should realise that God is there for us and that He will fight our corner if our motives are noble and true. When others throw stones, He stands beside us. We have no need to fear, to feel worthless or to feel alone.

What are the consequences of envy? These can only be loneliness and isolation, leading to bitterness. Who wants to spend time with someone who is insanely jealous? Let us be willing to shift the focus from what we want to trusting in God to provide what we need.

Let's replace any jealousy that seeps into our soul with an attitude of gratitude and appreciation.

Never Apologise for
Being Yourself

Mainly due to social media and Reality TV, we have become paralysed by our craving to be loved and accepted. What is happening when we scroll aimlessly through this vast entanglement of other people's lives? We can envy, admire, and ridicule such images and we can get obsessed with trying to be what we see others portraying themselves to be. Yet, when it comes to having imperfect lives, we are all the same.

None of us truly has it all together – it just looks like we have because there is a superficial filter for that. Throughout history, great men and women had the wisdom to realise that social acceptance and popularity were fleeting, and that Godly principles needed to be rooted in strengths greater than the passions, popularity, and the emotions of the times.

Never ever apologise for being yourself. Let everyone witness the authentic, imperfect, quirky, weird, beautiful, magical person that you are. It's not worth selling your soul for the sake of popularity. If we want to have true peace, we'll have to avoid people-pleasing and trying to be everyone's best pal. When we are just being ourselves, the right people will come into our life who will value, love, and accept us for who we are. Of course, that doesn't mean being bullish, self-centred, or insensitive – traits we can easily slip into – but rather, it means more about growing in humility, understanding and authenticity.

Walking on Eggshells is Not Our Father's Will

There's nothing worse than feeling we are walking on eggshells around someone. It seems that no matter what we say or do, it's picked up the wrong way or taken as criticism and always erupts in defensiveness, rage, silence, or storming off.

Are we dealing with simmering passive anger? Being confronted constantly with a ticking time bomb ready to explode? It's been said that walking on eggshells is usually a misguided attempt at preserving a doomed relationship. Over time, the eggshells become hard to break after walking on them for so long and, consequently, living in constant stress becomes the norm. We'll have to be strong in enforcing boundaries but at the same time be clear that the relationship as it was will be over – unless there is a dramatic change.

Ultimately, life is a gift from God above and too precious to spend walking on eggshells or tiptoeing through the tulips. The greatest conflicts in life are not between two people but between one discontented and embittered person and themselves.

Unlike some people, who we feel we are walking in eggshells around, our God is a God who loves us even if we mess up.

Our God is a God who accepts us even if we fail to measure up to perfection. Our God is a God who is patient with us in our sanctification and our growth in grace.

God is not easily irritated. God is not touchy. God does not throw tantrums. God is not quick to pull the trigger on us, rather the depth of God's heart is turned outward towards us in deep, intimate love, even when we fall short. We don't need to walk on eggshells around anyone and we definitely don't have to walk on eggshells around God.

A balanced inner calmness radiates only from a peaceful heart. It neither craves others' approval nor rejects others' presence. It neither pulls towards nor pushes away. This way, we'll have a reverent, respectful attitude towards life and everyone we meet. There is a calmness to a life lived in gratitude and appreciation and an inner joy.

As Jesus reminds us: "Blessed are the peacemakers, for they will be called children of God". (Matthew 5:9)

Bullying – The Pandemic of Our Times

There appears to be a myriad of myths and misconceptions surrounding the serious issue of bullying. Two of the main misconceptions are that bullying involves adolescents and that it's primarily about physical intimidation.

With cyber bullying becoming an ever-growing problem, now that most people have easy access to the Internet, targeting a victim can be done from anywhere in the world and from any number of subtle sources – in particular, through social networking sites, email, and text messaging.

Bullying tends to be an accumulation of many small incidents stretched over time. Each incident in isolation could seem trivial and not having grounds for serious concern, nor warranting disciplinary or legal action. But the drip-feeding of constant nit-picking, fault-finding and criticism with increasing regularity eventually identifies then unmasks the perpetrator. This defining moment occurs when the fall guy or girl realises that the ceaseless criticism represents bullying and has little validity. By discerning that "enough is enough" they then exercise their right not to be bullied anymore.

The stereotypical image of a bully is of a loud, brash, and domineering sort, but they are just as likely to be reserved, slightly withdrawn and insidious. There may be a grain of truth in their criticisms, but being so consumed with jealousy, anger, and contempt, they create a chaotic fractious and negative environment, losing all sense of rationality and fairness. They may use their charm and influence to entice the naïve or emotionally needy to follow them and support their witch hunt against their chosen target.

A serial bully moves from one target to another, perhaps working with another bully as a pair, or leading a pack. Bullies of all ages target people who are popular, vulnerable and in positions of influence. They have a subjective sense of right and wrong with no room for compromise or manoeuvre. They display a Jekyll & Hyde persona: Endearing and charming for much of the time but cruel and vindictive at other times – particularly when witnesses are absent.

Bullies isolate their targets with a view to disempower them – a beast-like tactic of control that is endemic to abusers. Abdication of responsibility and accountability is their hallmark. They are fully aware of the harm they are causing and cannot claim any measure of diminished responsibility but instead glean a twisted sense of satisfaction at seeing someone in distress.

The religious bully will arrogantly quote Scripture to flaunt perceived spiritual or intellectual superiority, whereas the school or building site bully may resort to physical intimidation. Alternatively, the corporate bully could stoop to sexual harassment or a vindictive whispering campaign.

But bullies from all backgrounds will always crave the last word with a view to stay in control. These individuals lack genuine empathy for others, with little concern for consequences, often feeding an egotistical craving to feel all-powerful. They may appear confident with high self-esteem, but this only conceals a brittle narcissism and a deep insecurity.

Human sensitivity comprises of a configuration of values to be cherished and nurtured, including empathy, respect, tolerance, dignity, honour, and consideration. Paul wrote: "For God did not give us a spirit of timidity, but of power, love, and self-discipline". (2 Timothy 1:7)

Those who lack sensitivity are themselves insensitive.

When confronted about bullying, the harasser will often claim their intended target is over-sensitive, paranoid, unwilling to accept criticism or simply playing the victim. After all, who wants to be tarred as a bully? Bullies may insinuate that their prey are weak and unstable, so that they themselves appear normal and balanced by comparison.

Anyone who is a victim of bullying should keep a written account of every time they were bullied. This can verify that they aren't isolated incidents, and that the harassment has been ongoing, making it easier to report the bullying in an objective, rational manner, giving no scope for the validity of the complaint to be questioned.

To continually violate the dignity of another person, in any shape or form, is to depart from the very basis of decent and reputable living. Intimidatory behaviour violates our Christian duty to love our neighbour as we love ourselves. In Matthew 5, Christ's teaching of "turning the other cheek" was counter cultural at the time, and it still is, but when applied to cases of bullying – whether it involves young or old – it misses the point of His original teaching.

When Jesus was slapped on the face by the guard of the High Priest, He did not turn his face so the guard could slap Him again. Instead, Jesus responded: "If I said something wrong, testify as to what is wrong. But if I spoke the truth, why did you strike me?" (John 18:19-23)

Jesus not only defended Himself with words, He confronted the bully and demanded an answer for his unjust treatment.

He doesn't want us to trade insults, nor does He want us to be consumed by revenge, but He does want the menace of bullying to be confronted and dealt with graciously and accordingly.

FORGIVE THEM, EVEN THOUGH THEY ARE NOT SORRY

Isn't forgiving incredibly difficult? Forgiving abuse? Forgiving betrayal? Forgiving slander against us? It seems almost obscene to forgive someone who has caused great harm to us or our families.

They may well have caused the first wound, but we, ourselves, are keeping the pain and misery going by seeking revenge and justice. This is what refusing to forgive does. Others may well have started it, but we refuse to let it go. Paul writes: "As Christ forgave us, so we must do the same". (Colossians 3:13)

Really, God? Get a grip! Do-you-actually-know-how-l-feel?

We think it's the perpetrators who made us feel this way, but if we won't forgive them, we continue to inflict the pain on ourselves. Forgiving is not being "soft". Forgiving is not even trusting that person again. Forgiving is being mature and gracious. Forgiving is not forgetting; it's being prepared to let go of the hurt and anger. To forgive is to set a prisoner free, and realise the prisoner was yourself. Forgive and let go, or bitterness and resentment will eat you alive.

Forgive, because we have been forgiven by the One who did no wrong. Jesus said: "Father, forgive them, for they do not know what they are doing". (Luke 23 v 34)

So, how on earth do we begin the process of healing? Well, for starters, keep no list of wrongs. Pray for our antagonists rather than plot against them. Hate the wrong without hating the wrongdoers. That sounds so simple but is so difficult to put into practice.

The reality is, we've all done and said things that caused disappointment and hurt to others, and shame and embarrassment to ourselves – whether we meant to or not. So, we too have needed forgiveness.

Does that make forgiveness easy? No, not at all. It has fits and starts, good days and bad, anger intermingled with love, irregular mercy spiked with moments of resentment. We make progress, only to take a wrong turn again. But it's okay: For as long as we're trying to forgive, we are making progress. It is when we no longer try to forgive that bitterness and rage kicks in. Keep trying, keep forgiving, because if we can't forgive it only keeps us embittered.

Forgiving doesn't mean forgetting about the wrong someone has done to you or trusting that person again. Nor does it mean that we've giving the message that what someone did or said was okay. It just means that we've let go of the anger towards someone, or the guilt towards ourselves. But that can be easier said than done. If forgiveness was easy, everyone would be doing it, but we clearly live in an unforgiving world. Let go, and let God deal with it.

Holding Grudges Only Keeps Us in Bondage

A letter reads:

Dear Frank. We've been neighbours for six stressful years. When you borrowed my three-piece ladder, it came back broken. When I was unwell, you blasted your heavy metal music all through the night. And when your dog pooped all over my freshly cut lawn, you just laughed. When my wig slipped off at the Christmas party, you refused to give me it back. I could go on, but I'm certainly not one to hold grudges. So, I am writing this letter to tell you that your house is on fire! Yours sincerely, Bob.

The reason Jesus taught us to forgive our enemies is not for their benefit but for our own. Holding a grudge against others seldom hurts them. They may well have forgotten about the issue we are still clinging on to. In some cases, it might even please them, if they are of that mindset.

It is never in our enlightened self-interest to hold grudges, regardless of whether it bothers the person we resent or not.

When it comes to hating, gossiping, ignoring, ridiculing, holding grudges, or seeking to cause harm – give it a break!

Liberation and spiritual freedom are the result of forgiving.

Grudges are simply for those who insist that they are owed something. Forgiveness is for those who are mature enough to move on. Grace, on the other hand, is for those who know they are owed something but choose to forgive and live a grudge-free life.

When we choose to be grace-centred, be someone who forgives and forgets and not hold grudges, we'd be leaving any revenge to the Lord.

We are reminded: Do not take revenge, my dear friends, but leave room for God's wrath, for it is written: "It is mine to avenge; I will repay," says the Lord. (Romans 12 v 19)

Never Borrow an Offence

This is called borrowed offence: Taking on someone else's grievance or taking someone's side in a dispute without knowing all the facts. I confess that I have fallen into that trap myself. After all, it's so easy to get swept away on the wave of judgement against someone when the source seems so sincere and plausible.

I once deleted someone on Facebook because of what I heard about him, from someone I thought I could trust, who spoke badly of the person concerned. I had a check in my spirit a few years ago and decided to get in touch with the person concerned but learned he had sadly passed away.

I love how the Message Bible puts it: "Don't eavesdrop on the conversation of others. What if the gossip's about you and you'd rather not hear it? You've done that a few times, haven't you – said things behind someone's back you wouldn't say to his face". (Ecclesiastes 7:21-22)

Let's never lend our heart to shunning, blocking, or disliking someone simply because someone else does. Plausibility doesn't always equate to truth. Surely, if someone chooses to judge or dislike someone that's up to them? There is no need for us to add to the spite-fest.

Let's also never judge someone's character based on the

words of someone else, especially if we have our own wee gripes and annoyances against the person being judged. Instead, study the motives behind the words of the person casting the bad judgement, and their track record. Always trust your discernment – trust your heart.

Pray for Those who Hurt Us

We can't control the way anyone responds to us. When it comes to the behaviour of others toward us, our hands are tied. We'll have to move beyond the naïve expectation that if we do good honourable people will always treat us right. The fact is, they may, or they may not. We cannot control how people respond to us.

We can only control how we respond. For as long as we think we can control people's attitude or behaviour toward us we are held in bondage by their opinions. If we think we can control or influence their opinion, and that opinion isn't positive, we will continue to feel demoralised, frustrated, and disrespected.

Be a warrior when it comes to fulfilling your purpose in life and be a saint when it comes to treating all people with respect, modelling love and compassion, and handling all snubs, rebukes, and slander with outright grace. It's easier said than done but we can ask Jesus to help us in the process.

Sadly, life is often a game with unfair rules and horrific, even fatal, outcomes.

Jesus didn't play the game and nor should we. In fact, He says: "Pray for those who hurt you". This is nothing to do with being soft or wimpy, this is an expression of his unmerited grace. Praying for someone involves asking good for them – not justifying their behaviour, but rather seeking the Lord's presence in their lives and praying for transformation of their hearts.

One of my heroes, Viktor Frankl, who lost practically all his family and every single possession during the Holocaust, said, "Everything can be taken from a man but one thing: The last of human freedoms – to choose one's attitude in any given set of circumstances, to choose one's own way".

Eradicating capital punishment does not mean killers will escape the ultimate judgement.

Every time we witness a high-profile case of a child who has been abducted, abused, or murdered, public feeling runs high with an understandable clamour for the re-introduction of the death penalty. This was the case in 2012, when 64-year-old Scottish born Robert Black was found guilty of the murder of nine-year-old Jennifer Cardy in Northern Ireland 30 years previously. Black was already serving 10 life sentences, imposed in 1994 after he was found guilty of killing three young girls in the 1980s.

Our moral conscience and desire for justice convince us that a price must be paid in proportion to the extremity of the crime as we view it. Many Christian denominations are against the death penalty because it denies the power of Christ to redeem, restore and transform all human beings. Their belief is that all human life is sacred and created by God, and therefore we must see all human life as significant and valuable, and that God Himself is the ultimate judge of all things. However, some crimes of unspeakable evil are simply beyond human forgiveness and redemption.

In John's Gospel (8:7) when the Pharisees brought a woman to Jesus who was caught in the act of adultery and asked Him if she should be stoned to death, Jesus replied, "If any one of you is without sin, let him be the first to throw a stone". This can be used by Christians to argue that Jesus rejected capital punishment in all instances. But was Jesus simply exposing the hypocrisy of the Pharisees who had no compassion for this woman?

I believe God allows capital punishment, although He lays down strict guidelines to keep judgement from being unfair or excessive.

> Punishment must be in proportion with the crime. (Exodus 21:23-25)
> Punishment must be based on certainty of guilt. (Deuteronomy 17:6)
> Punishment must result from premeditated intent. (Numbers 35:22-24)

This would appear to be a strong case for the likes of depraved serial child killers like Robert Black, Peter Tobin, and Ian Brady, to meet their fate this side of the grave, although all three have faced their day of judgement.

Both the Old and New Testaments indicate that personal retaliation is not appropriate. (Leviticus 19:18; Romans 12:19-13:7) Punishment should be the exclusive right of the government – not the man on the street. No matter how heinous the crime, retaliation, or vigilantism, as witnessed in murder of child killer Colin Hatch by a fellow inmate over ten years ago, it is contrary to biblical principles.

But our judiciary system is not infallible, because innocent people have been, and still are, wrongfully condemned. Stefan Kiszko, a tax clerk, was convicted of the sexual assault and murder of 11-year-old Lesley Molseed in Rochdale more than forty years ago. Kiszko confessed, following hours of police interrogation. Despite later pleading his innocence, he was mercilessly attacked and scalded with boiling water while in jail. Eventually he was freed after DNA evidence proved conclusively that he could never have committed the crime.

Black's repugnant callousness and lack of human feeling during his trial, emphasised by his yawning in court, heaped more misery on Jennifer's dignified family. Knowing he had information that the families and the police desperately sought gave Robert Black a twisted sense of power and control. Like Peter Tobin, he had no desire to ease his conscience and he clung on to the one thing that gave him power over the pain that his victim's families are suffering.

Mr Cardy said the family had prayed for Black in the wake of the guilty verdict, but that he believed his daughter's killer should pay the ultimate price for his crimes, when he added, "I would have to say that I would still say that somebody who commits murders like this, I believe their lives should be taken, I believe they should be put to death, that's my belief."

In a sense, Andrew Cardy got his wish as Robert Black finally relinquished all control here on earth in 2016 when his fate was decided by the Controller and Ultimate Judge of all things. Also, Mr Cardy took God at His word when he rightly said, "I've said many times that one of the lovely promises in the Scriptures is that the Lord gives a peace in this world that passes understanding".

Hate Less – Live Longer

Hate is something we have felt or experience at some point in our lives. However, if this negative emotion is not addressed it will inevitably drain our spirit and tarnish our soul. Frankly, our time here on earth is too precious and fragile to be sacrificed on wasted days combating the debilitating forces of hate, jealously, judgement and envy.

We may well use the expression "I hate you" in the spur of the moment when we are simply expressing anger. The danger, however, is that intense anger may indeed swell into a state that it can reasonably be labelled as "pure hatred". Our lack of grace and forgiveness allows us to hate, and our lack of compassion hardens our heart. Pride in our hearts keeps us resentful and keeps our mindset in a perpetual whirlwind of anger, resentment, and self-pity.

I remember, as a young loon around twelve years of age, watching the highlights of a Rangers v Celtic game on our old three channel black and white TV. The Rangers fans were singing about their hatred for Celtic and were full of armchair bravado. I joined in, only to be quickly rebuked by my stern-faced father, who told me in no uncertain terms never to hate anyone, not even a rival football team. So, lesson learned!

Nelson Mandela once said, "No one is born hating another person because of the colour of his skin, or his background, or his religion. People must learn to hate, and if they can learn to hate, they can be taught to love, for love comes more naturally to the human heart than its opposite".

I am not sure if hating less would extend our life, but I wouldn't be surprised if it did. However, I do know from experience that refusing to hate anybody, or anything, brings peace and acceptance into the forefront of our lives.

According to leading psychiatrists, hate is not a single, unified emotion. It is a blend of many other emotions, such as moral disgust, rage, resentment, and fear. But the components add up to what may ultimately come to feel like a single integrated emotion – an emotion that is overwhelmingly negative and very often exceedingly intense and volatile. When we feel it, there can be absolutely no doubt about what we are feeling.

So, let's not waste a single breath on feelings of hate or jealousy. Instead, let us show gratitude and thank God for granting us the spirit of grace and self-control. Let no one drag us to such a low, pitiful place in which we hate them.

"Above all else, guard your heart, for everything you do flows from it". (Proverbs 4 v 23)

THE VALUE OF UNITY CAN NEVER BE UNDERESTIMATED

Ask any pastor what they would most like to witness in the Church they lead, and we will find that 'unity within the congregation' would be high on their list.

God stands for, and affirms, the power of unity in getting things done. Speaking of the power of the people of Babel, the Lord said: "Behold, they are one people, and they have all one language, and this is only the beginning of what they will do. And nothing that they propose to do will now be impossible for them". (Genesis 11:6)

These people were united for the wrong reasons, yet God acknowledged what ability they had. Imagine what we can do if we are united for the right reasons. That's why the first thing that God did upon the establishment of the early Church was to give people a united language.

"The Holy Spirit empowered the believers to once again speak the same language". (Acts 2:8-11)

Unity itself is neutral until it is underpinned by good or bad motives. So, if Herod and Pilate are unified by their hatred and contempt for Jesus, as we read in Luke 23:12, this is not a good, healthy unity. But if Paul and Silas sing together in prison to glorify their Lord (Acts 16:25), this is a good unity.

Therefore, it is never enough to call ourselves followers of Jesus. To just have unity may be good or bad. The unified vote, more than sixty years ago in a church in Alabama, to forbid Blacks from attending services was not a good unity. In fact, it was appalling racial discrimination.

Spirit-rooted, grace-centred Christ-manifesting, truth-cherishing, humble-loving unity is designed by God to have at least two aims: To be a witness to the world, and to be an acclamation of the glory of God. Jesus makes the first of these most clear in John's Gospel. "A new commandment I give to you, that you love one another: just as I have loved you, you also are to love one another. By this, all people will know that you are my disciples, if you have love for one another". (John 13:34-35)

Unity is a wonderful thing in any area of life and can never be underestimated. In a culture saturated with pride, judgement, and envy, unity, teamwork, and camaraderie are powerful forces. In Church we hear so much about unity, but it's not Pentecostal unity or Reformed unity we should strive for – it's simply Church unity.

People who can work together, regardless of their personality, background, or irreconcilable differences will always succeed in the end. It's difficult to cultivate unity when there is clamour for position or an underlying critical or controlling spirit in God's house. We can quote the wonderful Psalm 133 and believe that when there is unity, God commands the blessing. But, at the same time, we cynically sneer at any expression of Church that is not our personal preference.

Familiarity can so easily bring contempt in even the strongest and a most respectful of alliances. We need togetherness, but in a way that we are joined at the heart, not at the hip. Let the heart be the organ that merges us with the spirit of grace to bring much needed unity in the Kingdom of God.

PERSONALITY TYPES

Why do opposites attract, then attack? Why are children so different in nature? Why are some of us people-orientated and others more task-orientated?

Personality Plus, a book I read almost 30 years ago, really opened my eyes to the differences in personalities and how we could understand each other much better.

Author Florence Littauer reveals how to determine what type of temperament we fall into: Popular Sanguine, Powerful Choleric, Perfect Melancholy, or Peaceful Phlegmatic. She opens the book by saying, "I was instantly fascinated with the four temperaments that originated with Hippocrates four hundred years before Christ was born".

Alternatively, George Selig and Alan Arroyo have identified more than sixteen hundred personality types, but I have narrowed them down to the four as they are described by Littauer: Ruler (Choleric), Promoter (Sanguine), Server (Phlegmatic), and Designer (Melancholy).

The names to describe behavioural and personality styles may change, but the characteristics of each style alter very little.

Sometimes we may think that others are just trying to be difficult. Often, these clashes or conflicts are no more than a matter of viewing things differently and not personal issues at all.

We also react differently to different people. Sometimes we instantly feel a connection with someone, and we are almost kindred spirits, as if we've known them for years. On the other hand, after only five minutes with someone else, we may start to feel irritated, uneasy, as we seem to be on an entirely different wavelength.

When we say: "it's just the way I am" to justify our behaviour, then we are, in a sense, eschewing responsibility for our actions. Although we are all created with a strong distinctive personality, we can mature and adapt and modify our nature to become more rounded and adaptable to other personality types and situations.

However, it takes humility and patience to exercise this. Once we understand that people don't always deliberately go out of their way to irritate us, make things awkward for us, or hurt us, it will change the way we look at people and how to deal with them.

We are a combination of all personality styles in varying degrees, but usually one will be more prominent than others. It's worth appreciating that each style has its strengths and weaknesses. Our weaknesses can teach us as much as our strengths if we are humble enough to accept them, and no one style is better than another.

By studying Scripture, we can see a diverse range of personalities. Whether it is Paul with his dominating Choleric nature (Acts 9:3-19), Peter's sanguine impulsiveness (John 21:1-22), Abraham's supportive phlegmatic trait (Genesis 12-22), or Moses' melancholic behaviour (Exodus 3-4).

Our greatest example in Scripture is when Jesus adapted His approach to His listeners. He used one approach with the Pharisees (direct and to the point), a differently style when He related a parable (learning through example), a different one again when He walked the streets and spoke to the woman at the well and answered the question of the young rich ruler.

He adapted His style and approach with each of His disciples, from being patient to being very direct. Each one was treated differently but loved no less. This approach is our key to better understanding and learning to adapt our own individual style, so that we are better understood, while not changing our essence or nature.

While each of us has a dominant style of interaction, we can adapt to each other's styles through practice and patience. Most relationships are stained or ended not by major differences but by small misunderstandings and basic personality differences. With grace, understanding and an awareness of personality differences, relationships can be healed, and people reconciled.

In Proverbs 25:11, we read: "A word fitly spoken is like an apple of gold in a setting of silver". Unfortunately, we can't change others, despite our efforts. We can, however, adapt our own approach to influence others and harmonise with them. It's reassuring to realise that we can be capable of adjusting our styles of interaction without changing the essence of who God created us to be.

We were created to live in relationship with others. "Do to others as you would have them do to you". (Matthew 7:12)

We learn this also in Christ's two great commandments.

Firstly: "You shall love the Lord your God with all your heart, and with all your soul, and with all your mind, and with all your strength".

Secondly: "You shall love your neighbour as yourself". (Mark 12:30-31)

There is no other commandment greater than these.

CRITICISM – FROM A CARING HEART OR A SPITEFUL MOUTH

Criticism is never enjoyable. If it is necessary to give criticism, it should only be constructive and given out of love. Too often, though, it is given in anger, spite, or out of plain ignorance. In a sense, if criticism is warranted, it fulfils the same function as pain in the human body – it calls attention to things that are not quite right. Criticism based on hearsay is not helpful; that is simply gossip.

If I hear that a person I respect, or someone who is careful and thoughtful is criticising me, my family, my Church, or my ministry, then naturally I want to ask myself if they see something that validates their view and justifies their criticism.

And certainly, with valid or measured criticism, or regarding serious criticism from people who are rightly aggrieved, I would listen, act upon it, learn from it and endeavour to grow. There is also a lot of criticism that doesn't seem to demand that kind of careful attention, though, if the person is reacting out of malice or judgementalism. To be honest, I see some Christians being led by spite, rather than spirit.

It seems to me that there are four kinds of criticism we can encounter:

Criticism that is deserved and is given in genuine kindness and concern.

Criticism that is deserved but given in a harsh and belittling way.

Criticism that is not deserved but is given in kindness and goodwill – a genuine, honest mistake.

Criticism that is undeserved, given in a harsh and demeaning way, and may have spite and ill will behind it.

If we are being honest, we'll admit that we have given out and received at least some of these forms of criticism.

From experience, I have found that uninformed criticism normally ends up exposing or embarrassing the critic when the truth is revealed. (Proverbs 18:13)

The self-righteous Pharisees criticised Jesus, based on their own faulty standards. Truth was not on their side. Correction is to be gentle. It comes from love, not from a sour, embittered nature.

In Galatians 5:22-23, we are reminded that the Spirit wants to produce in us love, joy, peace, patience, kindness, goodness, faithfulness, gentleness, and self-control. If criticism cannot be expressed in keeping with the fruit of the Spirit, it's better left unsaid.

The reality is, there is no defence against criticism, or avoidance of criticism, except obscurity or doing zilch under the safety of the parapet.

Throughout the years, I have been told that I am too nice to be a Church pastor and too impulsive to lead a Church.

I have also been told I am too soft to be in ministry, oh, and I have been labelled "controlling" by people who threw a tantrum when they found out I wasn't as soft as they had thought.

Who knows, there may be an element of truth in any or all these criticisms but, by the grace of God, after 11 years I am still leading a local Church.

Yes, I am deeply flawed, and I don't always get things right, but to the God I serve I am fearfully and wonderfully made and made in His image – and so are you!

Why, then, do we get our spiritual knickers in a twist when someone criticises us or clearly doesn't like us?

We will always be too forward, too full of ourselves, too drole, too religious, too nice, too outspoken, too irritating, too deep, or too quiet to some people.

The reality is: We will never be everyone's cup of tea; we are not called to be, but, believe me, when virtues are pointed out first, flaws seem less insurmountable.

Reality TV is the place where we win popularity contests, not the Kingdom of God. Let's face it, we can all have a bit of a "marmite" effect on certain people, but so what? I find marmite revolting but it still sells extremely well!

Our love and acceptance need to look past those who don't love and accept us and who seem to look for any opportunity to undermine us, belittle us, or put us down. We do not need to dislike them in return, however tempting or justified we feel. Instead, we should treat them with love and compassion – and not through gritted teeth. We'll simply love them, despite their lack of respect, their critical spirit, resentment, envy, or judgement they might have towards us.

We repay them with love, not because they deserve it, but because we refuse to become embittered. And because, like us, they need forgiveness.

Let us be encouraged that we will be just right – even perfect – for the people who love and accept us for who we are.

Imperfect Christians – Perfect God

Christians – perfect people? Absolutely not! Hypocritical? More than likely! Aren't we all at times? A perfect mess? You bet! Yet God uses us "warts and all" for His glory. A surprising and welcome discovery of the Bible is this: God uses misfits, oddballs, and failures. God knows everything about us, including our ugly parts, broken parts, and dysfunctional parts. Yet, He still believes in us; He still has a future and a hope for us.

Don't allow past failures to haunt you or hold you back. Many people think they could not follow Christ because of their past and because they are not good or holy enough. We look at others and mistakenly assume they have it all together, while the reality is that they, too, have their failures and insecurities.

We constantly analyse and scrutinise one another. We compare others to our standards – spoken or unspoken – to see how they measure up, after which we subconsciously accept or reject them. We praise them or criticise them; we revere them or ridicule them. We all secretly administer exams in the university of our own opinions.

God doesn't do that. He treats us all as equals.

Many of us were taught that God would only love and accept us, if, and when, we change, but, in fact, God loves us so that we can change. And God will still love us if we never change. What empowers change, what makes us desire change and transformation, is the experience of love, underpinned by amazing grace. It is that inherent experience of unconditional love that becomes the catalyst for change.

We live in a world saturated in sin and as a result we live lives that are less that squeaky clean. No one is perfect. No one is infallible. We may portray perfection and infallibility yet in reality fall short.

One of the great wonders of the Gospel is that God uses imperfect people to spread His glory. Since mankind first took a step outside the Garden of Eden, God has been calling the broken, the faithless, and the poor in spirit to do great things in His name. Just read the Bible if you don't believe me.

Even though my own life is blighted by countless mistakes, I refuse to rummage through my personal dung heap of failures and disappointments. I will admit to them, and l will repent, if necessary.

I will endeavour to correct my mistakes. I will press on. And you can too.

Buried or Planted?

Sometimes, when we find ourselves in a dark place, it feels like we have been buried, but we've simply been planted somewhere unfamiliar where we shall eventually flourish. It is often in what seems like our darkest times that the birth pains of breakthrough become evident.

Valley experiences shape us and mould us, but when we are going through them it is difficult to see hope for the future. These character-building experiences are often the preparation for a new productive season in our lives. Even this season, in which I am struggling with health, I find myself excited about the future with a real passion for writing this book, for travelling, and for my work in our local Church, among other things.

Overthinking – The Art of Creating Problems that Don't Exist

I have come to realise that anxiety and overthinking tend to go hand in hand. One of the deadly hallmarks of any type of anxiety disorder is the tendency to overthink everything. The anxious brain is hyper vigilant, always on the lookout for anything it perceives to be dangerous or threatening. This can sometimes be a good thing, if our discernment is accurate and healthy, but not if we tend to be suspicious of everything and everyone.

When we adopt a paralysis of analysis as an approach to everything, we can create problems where there aren't any. Obsessing over what we should say or should have said, what we did or should have done can drive us almost insane. Paranoia kicks in, and even the most trivial of things get magnified.

I have learned from often painful experiences that many misunderstandings in this world can be avoided if we would simply take the time to ask: "What else could this mean?" A high percentage of what we worry or obsess about either can't be changed or won't happen.

I know I am overthinking when my thinking is motivated by fear or driven by some unhealthy controlling compulsion. If I feel insecure in my acceptance with God, and I believe that thinking more clearly about the Christian life will make me more acceptable, I am overthinking. I need a kick up the backside and a good dose of the gospel of grace!

If we find ourselves driven to meticulously think through every little choice in our life in a kind of obsessive-compulsive way, we are clearly in the grip of something very unhealthy. Healthy thinking needs to flow from the heart of a restful reliance upon the mercy of God in Christ, so that we are not trying to justify ourselves by thinking, but rather, with the peaceful outworking of a heart that is fixed on Christ, we are doing what love calls for.

Self-evaluation can be healthy, especially when it helps us evaluate the condition of our heart, when it helps us see the truth or find that we have deviated off track. When introspection pulls us down into despair, it's no longer self-examination but, what Martyn Lloyd-Jones calls, morbidity. This morbidity makes us focus all our energies on ourselves, making us self-centred – the opposite of what Christ called us to do when He taught us to put others before ourselves.

Being Forgotten About Is Worse than Being Talked About

If there is anything in the world worse than being talked about, it must be being discarded or totally forgotten about. I clearly recall hearing a seasoned pastor telling us that, as a young Salvation Army officer, the first funeral he was asked to lead was for an old lady who only had one mourner. It struck me that there are people who don't just live lives of desperation, but also of loneliness and isolation. Some, of course, may choose such an existence, but not all. Jesus says He will never leave us or forsake us, and that's so true but we, too, must never neglect showing care and compassion to those around us who might not look good, smell good or fit effortlessly into our social circle.

Let's be kind and considerate in these increasingly challenging times.

Following Christ is a Call to Obedience Not Rebellion

No teenager in rebellion against his parents or the world seems able to resist Che Guevara's alluring image. Simply wearing a Che T-shirt is the simplest and most effective way of appearing to be on the right side of credibility. After all, try walking into your local pub wearing a T-shirt displaying your devotion for Christ, alongside your best friend who is wearing the familiar black and red Comrade Che one, and you'll find that there will most likely be two entirely different reactions by your peers.

Undoubtedly, there are attributes to admire about the cause Comrade Che stood for but perhaps in these times, with so many orphan hearts and shifting identities and alliances, the fantasy of an adventurer who crossed borders and broke down boundaries, without once betraying his basic loyalties, provides the restless youth of today with an icon that appeals to their roving impulses. For those who will never follow in his footsteps – submerged as many of them are in a world of cynicism and pessimism – nothing could be more admired than Che Guevara's contempt for material comfort and capitalist desires.

Guevara was certainly fervent about helping the less fortunate people in Latin America. He also opposed materialism and sought little for himself. But, unlike Christ, these goals appeared unachievable without bloodshed and violence.

Che Guevara held little regard for life. For him, bloodshed was required if a fairer world was to come to pass. He judged that the people of the developing world would be better served under socialism than capitalism. He may well have been right, although no "ism" is infallible, or incorruptible. Guevara's execution in Bolivia, as a relatively young man, made him a secular Messiah; the man who took upon himself the sins of the capitalist world and gave his life for the cause of the oppressed.

Ultimately, following Jesus Christ is a call to obedience, not rebellion. Rebellion is only a virtue when it occurs as an unintended by-product of obedience to Christ Himself. If it has anything at all to do with our ego or pride, rebellion becomes, at best, a distraction and, at worst, a sin.

Responding to the case of a Christian who was spared the sack for exhibiting a small cross on the dashboard of his van by his Marxist boss, who proudly displayed a picture of Guevara on his office wall, Journalist Peter Hitchens rather graphically and ghoulishly makes this assertion: "There are two rival forces that compete for supremacy in what was once a Christian country – the Gospel of Che, hot with hate and splattered with other people's blood and brains in the pursuit of a utopia that never comes. And the Gospel of Christ – a life laid down willingly for others".

While this may appear to be a brutal assessment of Guevara's life, it's in stark contrast to the Gospel of Christ, which is so often misunderstood and thus misrepresented. In essence, Che Guevara continues to be seen as a revered, as well as reviled figure, whereas Christ remains a revered and ridiculed historical figure.

Jesus Christ, who some may perceive as a distant religious figure, has had an overwhelming impact on people of almost a third of this planet who follow him – not because He was fashionable or ruthless, like Che Guevara, but because He brought a brave new way of life to this world that is still being embraced more than 2000 years after His death.

Embracing Our True Self
and Life of Adventure

It took me around three decades to figure this out, although I did have my doubts along the way: True strength does not come out of machoism or bravado – anything but!

Until we are broken and humbled the chances are that we will remain self-centred, self-reliant, and our strength will always be our own. For as long as we keep deceiving ourselves, we will be only of ourselves, wondering: What will we need God for?

But when we belong to Christ, we are part of something bigger than ourselves.

I am wary of a man who hasn't truly suffered; I won't let a man get really close to me spiritually who hasn't suffered a deep emotional wound. I wear my heart on my sleeve and struggle with believers, particularly Church leaders, who fake infallibility and perfection.

Think of the people you know, believers or non-believers, and ask yourself the question: Are they the kind of men or women I would be able to call at 3 am for help, when life is caving in around me? I can honestly say, I have among my friends and acquaintances more non-believers, or at least folk with no visible faith, that I know I could comfortably call.

Why is that I wonder?

Not only do I value trust and loyalty in my life, but I also value deep, soulful truth, and that can only come when a man or woman has walked the road of adversity – possibly even betrayal – and become real and vulnerable. That is when someone can be truly counted on.

The truth is, most of us are faking our way through life, avoiding conflict and true adventure. We pick only those battles we are sure to win, only the challenges we are sure we'll be able to handle, and those girls, who make our heart pound, in bars, Churches, and the workplace, we feel sure we can rescue.

Every human being carries a wound; I have never met a man or woman without one, although some wounds are more visible than others. No matter how good our lives may seem to us, we live in a broken world full of broken people.

John Eldridge writes: "Every boy, in his journey to become a man, takes an arrow in the centre of his heart, in the place of his strength. Because the wound is rarely discussed and even more rarely healed, every man carries a wound. And the wound is nearly always given by his father".

I am not sure if that is entirely true for everyone. It was for me but, in your case, it may have been a teacher, a so-called friend, an ex-boss, a Church pastor, or someone you deeply loved romantically.

The Big misconception in the Church today is that we are nothing more than "sinners saved by grace" but we are so much more than that if we are a new creation in Christ.

The New Testament calls us saints and holy ones.

The Old Testament reminds us that we are "fearfully and wonderfully made".

You are a son of God.

In the core of our very being we are all capable of great good and pure evil. Yes, there is a relentless war raging within us, but it is a civil war. The battle is not between us and our Creator; no, there is a traitor within who wars against our identity fighting alongside the Spirit of God in us: He is the one who comes to kill, steal, and destroy.

Of course, if you have not welcomed this invisible but clearly present God, the Spirit of Christ, you may not know what I am talking about. When God lives and breathes in us, we are delivered from that dead life.

The real you, and the real me, are on the side of God battling against our false self, and accepting this makes all the difference in the world.

Facing Discouragement in Ministry

In his powerful and challenging book *Though I walk through the valley* Dr Vance Havner tells of an old preacher who worked through the night to finish a sermon for his tiny congregation. His wife asked him why he spent so much time on a message he would share with so few. The pastor instantly replied, "You forget, my dear, how large my audience will be". Dr Havner added, "Nothing is trivial when heaven is looking on". He was so accurate, of course. We should raise our game when we remember who is looking on from the grandstand.

Discouragement clouds the mind and is often rooted in pride. We can allow fear, doubt and feelings of failure and inadequacy to derail us from fulfilling our calling and reaching our true potential.

I vividly recall, several years ago when I was in Tenerife, e-mailing one of our leadership team in the Church asking how the service had been on the Sunday. I was told it had been really good – the Word had been inspiring and the worship excellent – but there were few people present. Well, instead of thanking the Lord for the worship and the Word and those who were present, I felt so discouraged about the lack of numbers that I spend the rest of the day feeling deflated.

But, as I sat in my apartment later that evening, I was led to Joshua Chapter 1 verse 9, where I read: "Have I not commanded you? Be strong and courageous. Do not be afraid; do not be discouraged, for the Lord your God will be with you wherever you go".

While reading this I suddenly felt a surge of hope and optimism move through my body. I have since come to realise that true faith and durability in leadership must always pass the test of discouragement and disappointment.

It was also a wake-up call to me, as I had lost my primary focus and taken my eyes off what really mattered. When we feel discouraged, it helps to take time alone with the Lord and allow Him to examine our hearts and our motives.

Putting Failure into Proper Perspective

We are often too quick to judge isolated situations in our lives and label them as failures, instead of viewing the bigger picture in whatever we are going through – be it a relationship break up, a business failure, or guilt stemming from the behaviour of a rebellious child or teenager, who goes off the rails. Wouldn't you agree?

Reminiscing can be positive if we focus on good memories. We'll find peace in what we have once enjoyed and accomplished. Alternatively, if being nostalgic means we are continually harking back to that fabled, rose tinted time – particularly if we now view our life to be a failure – then it is an empty, debilitating exercise, doomed to produce nothing but frustration and an even greater sense of failure. Obsessing over our failures will not change the outcome. In fact, it's more likely to snare us in an emotional doom-loop that disables us from moving on. We cannot change the past, but we *can* shape our future, leaving our debilitating, monopolising, painful thoughts behind.

If we only focus on particular events that happen in our lives, it will be wise to keep things in perspective. In that case, we will be able to share the philosophy of someone like the Apostle Paul, who said: "I have learned in whatever state I am, to be content". That was a remarkable admission, considering that Paul had been shipwrecked, whipped, beaten, stoned, and imprisoned. Throughout everything his faith enabled him to maintain perspective. Paul realised that if he was doing what God called him to do, being labelled a success or failure by others would be irrelevant. This resilient attitude was endorsed when he wrote: "I can do all things through him who strengthens me". (Philippians 4:13)

The Bible recognises that we humans do fail: "We all stumble in many ways. If anyone is never at fault in what he says, he is a perfect man, able to keep his whole body in check". (James, Chapter 3 Verse 2)

My own life is littered with failure, but I have always been a risk taker and I believe God has granted me tenacity and persistence, particularly in relationships and ministry. Quite often God has lifted me out of the darkest and deepest depths of despair with His love, grace, and mercy, to restore me and put me back on track.

According to former American president Calvin Coolidge, nothing in this world can take the place of persistence. Talent will not; nothing is more common than unsuccessful men with talent. Genius will not; unrewarded genius is almost a proverb. Education will not; the world is full of educated derelicts. Persistence and determination alone are omnipotent.

And John Maxwell cites unwillingness to change, negative attitude, weak commitment, poor people skills, and relying on talent alone as some of the core reasons why people fail.

Fear of failure is rooted in our fear of being judged and losing the approval of people we respect and who we want to like us. We over concern ourselves by what people say about us. While accepting advice from the right people is healthy, we can give too much credibility to the opinions of others, who don't necessarily have our best interests at heart and douse our passion and confidence, undermining our ability to ultimately succeed.

Unless we cocoon ourselves in a reclusive existence, failure is unavoidable.

JK Rowling said, "It is impossible to live without failing at something, unless you live so cautiously that you might as well not have lived at all, in which case you have failed by default".

Or to quote comedian Woody Allen, "If you're not failing every now and again, it's a sign you're not doing anything very innovative".

As a wise man once said: "Lord, deliver me from the man who never makes a mistake, and also from the man who makes the same mistake twice."

It's Worth Considering

The house that is now looking a bit run down or dated is the dream home for someone who doesn't have a roof over their head.

That kid, who constantly angers and frustrates us, is the deep longing of a couple who have been told they can't have children.

That same job, that does our head in because of a boss who takes us for granted, is the desire of someone who is genuinely looking for employment.

The same partner or spouse, who often appears disorganised, disinterested, and insensitive but who is also loyal, honest, and committed, is the person God has brought you together with for a reason.

That unexpected diagnosis, that has left your life in turmoil, can be the catalyst for reprioritising life and appreciating what is important.

Life is never perfect, but it is seldom as bad as we think it is, if we remember to count our blessings and face life with a grateful heart.

THE VALUE OF TRUE FRIENDSHIP

In Ecclesiastes 3:10, we are reminded that two are better than one, because they have a good reward for their toil; if they fall, one will uplift the other.

But have you ever believed to be in a lifelong friendship with someone, only to be betrayed or simply being taken for granted along the way? Even the best of friends can have disagreements and fall outs, but these are things that run much deeper.

I have slowly come to realise that an acquaintance merely enjoys or tolerates our company. A fair-weather companion flatters us when all is well – and they are ten a penny.

But a true friend has our best interests at heart; he or she has the guts to tell us what we need to hear, and even ignores or disregards any gossip they hear about us. They are that friend we know we can call at 3am when everybody else is sound asleep. Their opening words will more often be: 'How are you?' than 'Can you do this for me?'

They know the worst of us but choose to focus on the best of us. Genuine friendship is agenda free and the only rose we will ever come across without thorns. Loyal friends are few and far between, but they are priceless. We all have a friend during each season of life, but we are truly blessed to have the same friend in all stages of life. In fact, we are doubly blessed to have more than one! The phrase "loyal friend" conjures up a powerful sense of belonging and solidarity. With it comes the idea of wholehearted fidelity, coupled with unswerving devotion and faithfulness.

Never has this wonderful quote by Henry Nouwen been more evident in my life than since my MND diagnosis: "When we honestly ask ourselves which persons in our lives mean the most to us, we often find that it is those who, instead of giving advice, solutions, or cures, have chosen rather to share our pain and touch our wounds with a warm and tender hand. The friend who can be silent with us in a moment of despair or confusion, who can stay with us in an hour of need, grief, and bereavement, who can tolerate not knowing, not curing, not healing and face with us the reality of our powerlessness, that is a friend who cares." Henri J.M. Nouwen: *The Road to Daybreak: A Spiritual Journey.*

Bossiness Is Not Leadership

Controlling, or aggressive behaviour in childhood comes in many forms: Defiance, stubbornness, and bossiness, to name a few. It is probably safe to say that as children we expressed ourselves in one of these ways, at least occasionally. The real danger, of course, is that bossy and controlling behaviour remains with us into adulthood if we don't mature, even if more subtly disguised.

Bossiness is not leadership. In fact, bossiness is the opposite of leadership. Being bossy is a skill that every 3-year-old bairn has mastered. Bossy is: "Shut up and do it my way; I know best!" but leadership is the opposite. Leadership is: "Follow me, not by what I say or threaten, but by my Christ-like example".

Bossy wee girls can be queen bees with their little minions following them. This mimics leadership, but it's not. Queen bees attain their positions of power by tearing others down through instilling fear and intimidation. Bully boys can be miniature Rambos or over-grown action men with their impressionable sidekicks in tow. They attain their positions of power by intimidation and instilling fear, with subtle threats of physical retribution thrown into the mix.

At any age, both sexes can be masters of manipulation and not so gentle persuasion. But if you have ever been a victim of one of these "bossy girls" or "bully boys" you know that this isn't true leadership. In fact, it's not even acceptable human behaviour. Treating others with dignity, grace, respect, and compassion is not just the requirement of leaders, it's expected from us all.

Jesus dictated to us not only what is God-honouring, but also what is effective when people are looking for authentic leadership. They are not looking for people who are on an ego trip, on the war path or who crave a big following to keep their ego satisfied, they are looking for people who have been satisfied by Jesus. He is their identity, and they want others to experience that. Ultimately, they are willing to stoop down low. They are willing to be patient. They are willing to wait. They are willing to serve.

Most people are drawn to humility, authenticity, and grace. Most are willing to get behind somebody like that.

No One Is Above Reproach

The sad and disturbing findings of the investigation commissioned by the RZIM global organisation into the behaviour of its late founder Ravi Zacharias has once again highlighted the deep pain and suffering caused by emotional, spiritual, and physical abuse.

Following the death of Zacharias, the then American Vice President, Mike Pence spoke at his memorial service, lauding him as a great evangelist "armed with intellect, girded with truth and love", only for this to be countered several months later by Carson Weitnauer, a former RZIM employee, who referred to Zacharias in response to allegations as: "one of his generation's greatest frauds", "a sexual predator", and a "uniquely charismatic manipulator".

As someone who was an avid follower of Zacharias's ministry for many years I, like many others, was shocked, saddened and deeply challenged to witness the posthumous fall from grace of a heralded Christian apologist. I certainly don't feel led or even qualified to dissect the whole tragic case and appoint myself judge and jury over the story that has sent shockwaves through the Christian world. But I do feel qualified to share on control and manipulation in general, which rears its repulsive head in all walks of life.

When a Christian leader, or anyone else, comes across as controlling and arrogant, it may be simply because that's what they really are. Pride and arrogance weren't the first things most of us saw in Ravi. What we saw was apparent humility and devotion to Jesus. When these qualities are the genuine fruit of God's Spirit, they are beautiful; when they are not, they can become tools to manipulate others into gratifying our sinful desires.

Time and time again, Scriptures remind us that we gain nothing by making someone else suffer for our own good or to satisfy our own insatiable desires.

Half of deceitful people lie with their lips, the other half with their tears. If we are an approval addict, our behaviour will be as easy to control as that of any other addict. All a manipulator needs to do is implement a simple two-step process: Give us what we crave and then threaten to take it away, and they'll have us trapped.

Control creeps up on us. It doesn't happen overnight, and it often operates under the radar. The manipulator will shock with both a lack of empathy and a grandiose sense of entitlement, as well as threats of character assassinations when their control is challenged. Pathological rage of the most sadistic kind, devoid of any morsel of empathy, often becomes evident when the controller fears they are being unmasked and are losing control.

The measure of a man or woman is how they handle being in a place of responsibility or authority. Some become demi-gods, while wise ones learn to humbly rely on God. The Apostle Paul wrote to the Church in Ephesus with this advice, which is also a warning to those who manipulate and deceive: "Let no one deceive you with empty words, for because of such things God's wrath comes on those who are disobedient." (Ephesians 6 verse 5)

Paul recognises our weaknesses but, more surprisingly, he recognises his own: "I cannot understand my own behaviour. I fail to carry out the things I want to do, and I find myself doing the very things I hate. When I act against my own will, that means

I have a self that acknowledges that the Law is good, and so the thing behaving in that way is not my self but sin living in me". (Romans 7 verse 15)

And this was the same Paul who wrote more than half the New Testament!

Lord, have mercy upon us all.

God is Looking for
Servants, Not Celebrities

God is looking for servants, not celebrities. He is also looking for big hearts, not just popular personalities. Charles Hadden Spurgeon was an absolute phenomenon of his time, preaching to over ten million people in his lifetime. During each service, stenographers eagerly recorded his message. At the end of every night the sermon was sent to print to be sold in shops and railway stations the next morning. Yet, for all his anointing and influence, Spurgeon was a humble man.

There was nothing superficial or showy about him. He approached Scripture on his knees. He seemed to have a deep awareness that he had been called by the grace of God and that it was that same grace which empowered and equipped him for the privilege of ministry. This genuine humility of heart allowed him to realise he could plant and water, but only God could make things grow.

We live in a celebrity culture that has sadly also infiltrated the Christian Church. Every few months a big Christian personality hits the headlines for all the wrong reasons because he is not willing to keep his lustful tendencies, his greed for money or his inflated ego in check. Let's not kid ourselves: It is not what people say about us or what we say about ourselves that matters, but rather what God knows about us when we don't have an audience or a congregation.

Scripture reminds us of the fact that God deliberately chooses the despised, foolish, and weak to be His servants. In doing this, He confounds the mighty, proves His power and reveals who He really is.

"But God has chosen the foolish things of the world to put to shame the wise, and God has chosen the weak things of the world to put to shame the things which are mighty". (1 Cor 1:27)

Does God Still Heal Today?

Healing is a hugely sensitive subject. Today, as in the New Testament and throughout Church history, God's healing power is a reality that has touched many lives, yet we also see many whose prayers go seemingly unanswered.

There is a cruel and sickening myth that torments people who are ill and that is the notion that God wants to heal everyone, and that if we are not healed it is always our own fault for not having enough faith or that we harbour unrepentant sin. Of course, as someone who enjoyed good heath for many years, I probably did not give this massive issue enough thought or even enough Biblical or historical research.

I recall reading the disturbing story of a young couple with a brain-damaged four-year old son who died despite fervent prayers for healing. I was shocked when a well-known American celebrity pastor told the grieving parents: "I don't believe this was God's will. He didn't allow this to happen. It's either my fault, your fault, both of our faults, or things that we don't understand". According to the pastor: "The grieving couple prayed, and God showed them some areas where they had allowed fear, doubt, and unbelief in. This had hindered their faith and kept them from receiving the miracle they needed. Apparently, because they received the truth, they repented and were able to overcome that fear".

He Implied that the parents' sin of unbelief resulted in the death of their child. Furthermore, I believe there must have been far more people praying for the child's recovery than the scapegoated parents praying for their child's healing.

In reading that alarming story I would doubt that the grieving parents had a lack of faith. More like, they had both faith and uncertainty as most parents would have in such a dire situation. They were told that they were responsible and needed to repent. How cruel, devastating, and confusing for parents already grieving the loss of a child. There are indeed things that happen in this world that we don't understand.

All this raises an enormous question: If God wants all believers to be well, why are so many believers not well, either emotionally or physically? And why have many Christians throughout history, as well as in recent times not been granted long and healthy lives? Of course, we live in a fallen world where sin and sickness abound, but to tar people as sinful or lacking in faith is cruel and demoralising.

Joni Eareckson Tada struggled with this issue for a long time. As she recounts in her book *Joni*, she sought physical healing of her quadriplegia. She prayed and fully believed that God would heal her. In her words: "I certainly believed. I was calling up my girlfriends saying, "Next time you see me I'm going to be running up your sidewalk. God's going to heal me". Yet, Joni is still in a wheelchair today. More than fifty years after the accident that left her paralysed, God has not healed her. God hasn't healed Justin Peters (Cerebral Palsy since birth) or Cannon Andrew White (MS for over 20 years) either, but He continues to use them powerfully.

Joni's perspective is one of great faith and one that I totally agree with: "God may remove our suffering, and that will be great cause for praise. But if not, He will use it, He will use anything and everything that stands in the way of His fellowship with you".

Some feel that God will never heal anyone miraculously today. Many people are healed today, and He is still the God of miracles. Others are of the opinion that God will always heal a person if he or she has enough faith. But God will not be put into either box.

Bethel pastor Bill Johnson, who lost his wife Beni, spoke these powerful and emotional words after her passing: "God is not a vending machine that I get to put a quarter into and withdraw from Him what I want. He chooses what He gives. But it is the wicked at heart that say 'God didn't do what I wanted. He is a liar'. May I never be found critiquing God when things don't go my way". This appeared to be a much welcomed and liberating U-turn away from quotes such as: "I refuse to create a theology that allows for illness".

The concept of divine sovereignty is often oversimplified. We tend to assume that, if God is not directly answering our prayers in the manner that we want, He can't truly be sovereign. Or that everything is His will, so there is no point in praying for healing. I even get the feeling I am a let-down or a disappointment to these believers, who believe God wants to heal everyone, because I am not yet healed. It challenges their twisted theology.

Isaiah 53:5, which is also quoted in 1 Peter 2:24, is a key verse on healing, but it is often misunderstood and misapplied, especially in word of faith and in health and wealth circles. "But he was pierced for our transgressions, he was crushed for our iniquities; the punishment that brought us peace was upon him, and by his wounds we are healed". The word "healed" can mean either spiritual or physical healing, but the contexts of 1st Peter chapter 2 make it clear that it is speaking of spiritual healing.

We do, however, see in Matthew 8:16-17 that the previous verse in Isaiah ("He took up our infirmities and bore our diseases") is quoted in the context of Jesus' healing and deliverance ministry. It seems that physical healing is available but that by far the most significant healing is spiritual. This 'spiritual healing' changes our condition before God for this life and, crucially, for all eternity.

It is my belief that most physical illness does not arise from personal sin, and Scripture cautions us against making glib connections between the two. We must make no assumptions, but original sin is the cause of all sickness. In certain circumstances, it can become clear that an illness is either part of God's disciplinary plan or simply a disregard for personal health. It is wise then to practice self-examination when we are suffering physical illness. When we become aware of specific sins we haven't been repenting of, it's appropriate to personally repent or to involve our Church elders in the way James outlines in chapter 5 of his epistle. Healing is not necessarily automatic but – much more importantly – forgiveness is.

Photos of empty wheelchairs or walking sticks leaning against a wall are no true indication that anyone has been healed either. As I write, my walking stick is leaning against the wall in my kitchen, but that proves nothing. I do believe, though, that God can physically bring paralysed people out of chairs and heal the lame, but it shouldn't be stage managed.

People who suffer need empathy and compassion, perhaps even those who have suffered themselves, to remind other sufferers that there is hope. As one minister who regularly prays for the sick puts it: "I can't guarantee that people will be healed when we pray for them, because I am not God. I can guarantee that people will be loved and respected when we pray because that is about how we treat them as we minister. That is our responsibility". We also see the remarkable compassion and professionalism shown by so many in the medical profession.

At the pool of Bethsaida Jesus went to one person who said he had no-one to help him into the pool. He healed only one in a huge multitude (John 5), yet we also see that His ministry was full of miracles, including miraculous healings.

It is right to accept responsibility to care and pray for others.

However, let us also accept in equal measure that we do not understand everything and that with our limited perspective we have no right to blame God or anyone else if we do not see the results we expect.

Ultimately, our full physical healing awaits us in heaven. In heaven, there will be no more pain, sickness, disease, suffering, or death. (Revelation 21)

THE DANDELION – A BLAND AND UNWANTED WEED

With my enforced retirement, I certainly have more time to slow down and reflect on many of the things I was always too busy to appreciate. Day dreaming hasn't really become a recent preoccupation for me, but it comes more naturally now!

During the summer of 1967 the Rolling Stones released a song with the line "Dandelion don't tell no lies, dandelion will make you wise" which, with its psychedelic sound, fitted seamlessly into the famous summer of love.

So, when I spot dandelions here in Scotland, I ask myself: "What really is a dandelion and how should we view it?" Well, I guess the answer is that it's a weed or a flower, depending on where it's growing, as well as our attitude towards dandelions. The dandelion is a bonny, yellow, smiling flower. Its bloom is a brilliant colour and has a wonderful texture, but many of us see it as no more than an unwanted weed. Most bland, unwanted things in this world have real value if we are willing to look a bit deeper.

Nowadays, the dandelion's old virtues are almost forgotten. Apparently, its self-blanched inner leaves are excellent spring greens, fresh or cooked. Its roots can be used for potherbs. They may be used for healing purposes, acting as a mild laxative, and its use can improve digestion, while it is also suggested that dandelions can be used as herbal remedies to improve liver and gallbladder function. Also, once upon a time wine was made from the bright yellow flowers and the dried and ground roots were a substitute for coffee. But this was all before the dandelion became nothing more than a backyard weed.

In the book of Numbers, God comforts the Israelites throughout the intense process of being delivered from Egypt with His promise to bring them to a land flowing with milk and honey. He pictures their future in a poetic way, relaying that the landscape would have plenty of forage for flocks, enabling herds to multiply and reproduce, resulting in milk to nurse their young. Clearly, the fields would be covered in wildflowers, enabling bees to find plentiful pollen, resulting in honey to feed new bees. Dandelions plant beautifully in the middle of this metaphor, with their nutritious green leaves for grazers and bright yellow flowers so inviting to pollinators.

No wonder God said in the first book of Scripture, "See, I give you every seed-bearing plant that is upon all the earth, and every tree that has seed-bearing fruit; they shall be yours for food". (Genesis 1.29)

Would it be reasonable then to suggest that a dandelion, one of those seemingly bland, common things we encounter every day, is really a thing of beauty? If only we have eyes to see.

Two Important Truths

If you are wheelchair bound or bravely fighting serious illness and have been constantly told you need to be "delivered" or simply "claim a healing", please be comforted and reassured by the truth that praying passionately for healing and accepting suffering with courage, positivity and dignity are both honourable acts of faith.

Football and Alcoholism – A Long and Complex Relationship

A forage into YouTube had me reflecting on the lives and careers of two Scottish football players of yesteryear, but whose careers were tragically blighted by alcohol.

Jim Baxter came to national and global prominence as a player for Rangers and Scotland in the early 1960s – a bit before my time. He was greatly admired for his stylish play, controlling the game with a seemingly "leisurely artistry" and refusing to conform with the "efficient" style that dominated British football in those days. But through time, Baxter's contempt for both authority and hard training became as strong as his irrepressible belief in his own ability. He frequently turned to drink as a way of escaping football's disappointments. And when his slim frame turned to flab and his legs gradually went, the genius was lost too.

When he died in 2001 at the age of 59, he was on liver number three. At his peak on the park, he was rightly regarded as one of the best players in the world, but tragically at his drinking peak he admitted he was consuming three bottles of Bacardi a day.

Sportswriter Gardner Spiers, perhaps unfairly and certainly insensitively, wrote this sobering inscription after his funeral: "For every heroic bar-stool story recounted last week, the pain and suffering never quite departed him. Through the long self-indulgent hours, week after week, year after year, Baxter first did in his family and then wrecked his own career".

In the mid-1970s, as a fitba daft teenager, I clearly remember George Connelly, the introverted, elegant, and gifted Celtic defender who turned his back on the game at only 26 years of age. Despite being managed by Jock Stein – one of the best Scottish football managers of all time, alongside Alex Ferguson, Matt Busby and Bill Shankly – Connelly continually walked out on the club, as he struggled to cope with fame and the pressures of the game.

Living modestly, while battling to conquer his personal demons, he was largely anonymous until the launch of his autobiography five years ago. In *Celtic's Lost Legend,* as well as sharing the exhilarating experiences of his career, he talks openly of his battle with alcoholism, which affected him for more than 30 years. As he does this, he exposes the crushing reality of the path that so many have gone down.

George lost both his parents, his sister, as well as a brother in alcohol-related deaths, which naturally prompts the age-old debate: Is alcoholism genetically inherited or is it simply down to lack of willpower and social environment, or perhaps even a combination of all these factors?

For the likes of Baxter and Connelly, there were no elite professional counsellors or state of the art rehab centres to help them conquer their demons.

At the height of their powers, depression was something they could just shake off with a few good performances or a good "bevy" out in the town with their mates. But for anyone, not just football players, when social drinking develops into comfort drinking it turns into a crutch that becomes ingrained in our very being. As prideful beings, it is incredibly difficult to admit that we are in the grip of an overwhelming and all-consuming addiction. After all, in Scottish culture it's much more credible to be viewed as a hardened drinker than to admit to anyone that we are struggling to cope.

In a refreshingly frank interview for the Scottish Herald in 2006, his interviewer observed that George Connelly, for all his accomplishments as a footballer, appeared cocooned in humility, refusing to bask in personal glory, whenever he was reminded of his great performances in a Celtic jersey.

When asked if he believed in God, George offered a strained smile before replying, "I knew you were going to ask me that. I was thinking about it before you came, and I knew you'd ask me they kind of things. That's a pass. It's private". A guarded response, typical of many football men who would rather be seen as having fallen from grace than saved by grace.

Bertrand Russell and the God He Dismissed and Ridiculed

Bertrand Russell was acknowledged as one of the greatest thinkers of the 20th century – a brilliant mathematician and philosopher. As a Nobel Prize winner for literature, he was a defender of humanity and freedom of thought. At times, Russell claimed to be an atheist. In his essay *Why I Am Not a Christian* he wrote: "I do not believe in God".

On other occasions, he simply settled for being an agnostic, yet, quite bizarrely, Russell did not mind being called a Christian. In another essay, discussing *Can an Agnostic be a Christian?* he wrote: "If you mean by a 'Christian' a man who loves his neighbour, who has wide sympathy with suffering, and who ardently desires a world freed from the cruelties and abominations that at present disfigure it, then certainly you will be justified in calling me a Christian".

Russell's views on religion and morality caused great anger in the early part of the 20th century. Yet, his writing smoothed a path for the general mood of anti-Christian rhetoric, so prominent today, led by eminent Biologist Richard Dawkins.

My Father - Bertrand Russell, written by his only daughter Katharine Tait, is a fascinating book in which she shares candidly and emotionally about having Bertrand Russell as her father. Katharine gives readers an intimate peek into the personal life of the great philosopher. Despite expressing anger, ambivalence, and frustrations, it is evident she loved her father immensely.

Russell was a fervent advocate of Darwinism. He taught his daughter that mankind was no more than an accident of evolution. When he travelled with his family, Katherine recalls: "He suggested that we might lean out the windows when we passed other cars and shout out: 'Your grandfather was a monkey'. "This," she said, "was to convince them of the correctness of Darwin's theory of evolution".

Russell, in essence, was practising child indoctrination – the very thing the New Atheist movement accuses Christians of doing. Katherine Tait also wrote: "When he wanted to attack religion, he sought out its most egregious errors and held them up to ridicule, while avoiding serious discussion of the basic message".

It is unsurprising, therefore, that the philosopher had such an adverse opinion of Christians. In his own autobiography he wrote: "The sea, the stars, the night wind in waste places, mean more to me than even the human beings I love best, and I am conscious that human affection is to me at bottom an attempt to escape from the vain search for God".

But according to Katherine, the esteemed intellectual kept on changing his views: "Christians were mocked for imagining that man is important in the vast scheme of the universe, even the high point of all creation – yet my father thought man and his preservation the most important thing in the world, and he lived in hopes of a better life to come".

Russell once said: "Human affection was but an attempt to escape the vain search for God". In a poignant piece of her book, his daughter concluded: "I believe myself that his whole life was a search for God. Indeed, he had first taken up philosophy in the hope of finding proof of the evidence of the existence of God. Somewhere at the back of my father's mind, at the bottom of his heart, in the depths of his soul – which he did not believe he had – there was an empty space that had once been filled by God, and he never found anything else to put in it".

Like many people these days, Russell, for all his great intellect, could never grasp the wisdom of Solomon in Ecclesiastes 3:11 – "He has made everything beautiful in its time. He has also set eternity in the hearts of men; yet they cannot fathom what God has done from beginning to end".

Accept the Encouragement but Pass on the Praise

One way of experiencing appreciation is through receiving genuine compliments and words of encouragement. Yet they are biodegradable; they dissolve in time. That's why we can always use another!

It could be argued that words are singularly the most powerful force available to humanity. We can choose to use this force constructively with words of encouragement, or destructively using words of judgement or unfair criticism.

I confess that my words are not always encouraging, so this is not something I claim mastery over. Too often I have spoken in haste – usually through frustration and impatience – and regretted what had come out of my mouth. To be honest, although my father was a good man, he never really encouraged me or gave much praise, and I think that is at least part of the reason why I have committed myself to being a real encourager, both in ministry and life in general.

It's not rocket science to realise that words have the power and potency to help, heal, hinder, hurt, harm, humiliate and humble. When we are free of envy, judgement, and cynicism giving encouragement becomes natural. Although the carnal clamour for constant praise can be like a narcotic craving for many, genuine encouragement is vital for us all.

As the late John Wimber said: "Accept the encouragement but pass on the praise".

FALSE MODESTY IS ROOTED IN PRIDE

I'm often asked what I do for a living. "So, you are a Painter?" and that was the cue for my standard reply: "Aye, I'm jist yer average run o the mill semi-skilled hoose painter"- until I was convicted of massaging my frequently bruised ego.

In truth, I was hoping they would say: "No, being a painter is a really good job! You must get a lot of job satisfaction!" A perfect response to my false modesty, enabling me to crank my low self-worth up a couple of notches – at least for about 10 minutes or so anyway!

When marriage counsellors ask: "What problems do you see most?" depression, anxiety, anger, and infidelity all make the cut. But the top answer may surprise you: It's pride; often disguised as false modesty but exposed as brittle narcissism. Pride being the chart-topper shouldn't come as a surprise to anyone; and least of all to Christians. After all, Proverbs 6:16–19 lists seven traits that God despises, and the very first – haughty eyes – is the proverbial way of talking about pride.

As seriously dangerous pride is, it's often equally hard to spot. When it comes to diagnosing our hearts, those of us who have contacted the disease of pride have a challenging time identifying the thorn in our own side. Pride affects our eyesight, causing us to view ourselves through a lens that colours and distorts reality. Pride will paint even our ugliness in sin and wrong-doing as beautiful and commendable.

We can't conclude that we don't struggle with pride because we don't see pride in our hearts. The comfortable "fuzzy" moments when I pat myself on the back for how well I am doing are the moments that should alarm me the most. I need to reach for the glasses of Christ-like humility, remembering that nothing good dwells in my flesh, and search my heart for secret pride and its symptoms. All self-exaltation is a re-crucifixion of Christ because he died to kill pride.

Of course, a sense of accomplishment is often good and healthy, and so is a well-deserved and sincere pat on the back, but if boasting is the result of any recognition or praise then pride is evident in our lives. Every boast and every spout of false modesty mocks the suffering of Jesus. Thankfully, though, every humble deed, every modest motive, every act of faith glorifies the grace of God in Christ.

Punctured Pride is Simply Counterfeit Humility

Failure is often the best but also the most painful way of humbling us. We are only human; creatures of clay with feet of clay, and occasionally, or maybe even frequently, we fall. But it's often easier just to feel punctured pride than true humility. Punctured pride says: How could this happen to me? while true humility says: I'm surprised this doesn't happen to me more often.

The tragic reality is that pride gets no real pleasure out of having, or achieving, something only through outscoring the next man or woman. It is the comparison that makes us proud; the fuzzy feeling of being above the rest, even for a short time. Once the element of competition and one-upmanship is gone, pride also dissipates – until the next time!

Being genuinely humble isn't a case of denying our strength – our gifts and talents will always be self-evident, so there's no need to enforce them on others. False humility is counterfeit humility; it is simply twisted pride. It rears its ugly head when we subtly build ourselves up while pretending to tear ourselves down or belittle ourselves to gain sympathy or praise.

A large part of being humble is being honest about our

weaknesses. True humility is staying teachable, regardless of how much we know or think we know.

"Grace puts its hand on the boasting mouth, and shuts it once for all" – Charles Spurgeon

Appreciating the Quiet Sensitive People Around Us

I have come across a lot of quiet people in my life; I have met them at school, in the pub, at the football, in Church and I have worked with a few. I have even gone out with one or two over the years. Quiet, sensitive people tend to shun the limelight and avoid controversy and confrontation. Although very normal and intelligent, their inner world is by default mysterious, quiet people are often wrongly assumed to be aloof, boring, or even weird.

I have learned never to underestimate the social awareness and sense of reality in quiet persons; they are generally some of the most observant, loyal, and dependable people I have ever met.

God loves all personalities, especially quiet servants.

They are the supporting cast of the kingdom.

They seek to do what is right, not what looks impressive.

They tend to serve in the background and never boast about their considerable talents.

They give gladly and, without telling anyone, support those who are sick or marginalised.

It was the servant spirit of Mary that led God to choose her to be the mother of Jesus. She was simple, trusting, and loyal. She said: "I am the servant of the Lord. Let this happen to me as you say". (Luke 1:38)

When God wants to bring Christ into the world, He looks for humble servants. No diploma, impressive family background, inflated ego, prestigious birthplace, or fat bank account is required. Let all you quiet, private, unassuming people be reminded of the fact that God can use you powerfully without the need for you to be the life and soul of the party.

Let's never assume quiet is weak and loud is strong.

Peace is More Important than Winning the War

This is certainly the case as we grow older. Proving a point or winning the argument is often only important to ourselves and our image. Of course, we need to stand up against betrayal, racism, bullying, abuse, and the like, but much of what we get on our high horse about is not worth the hassle.

A few days seem to pass quite smoothly without coming face to face with an uninvited, unanticipated, yet unavoidable decision. But like a wild untamed cat, these decisions spring upon us without warning. They disorientate and bewilder. A bolt out of the blue. Where did that come from? Whew!!! Suddenly, we are hurled into an air of uncertainty and only instinct will determine whether we will land on our feet or lose face. Our natural reaction is to react and respond.

I think most of us have been there. Insensitivity makes a wound heal slowly. If someone hurts our feelings intentionally, we generally know how to react for we know the source of the pain. But if someone accidentally bruises our soul, it's difficult to know how to respond.

Jesus says: "Peace I leave with you; my peace I give to you.

Not as the world gives do I give to you. Let not your hearts be troubled, neither let them be afraid". (John 14:27)

Through the years, I have frequently received biting, condescending comments on something I posted on social media. Some of these were clearly an attempt to bait or inflame, and although my initial reaction was to respond, over time I wisely decided to ignore them or respond privately. Ignoring criticism or clear attempts to antagonise was never easy for me while growing up, and even well into adulthood. I was impulsive, as well as quite volatile, although not in a physically aggressive way.

We are aware of our own weaknesses and so do those who attempt to press our buttons, as does the one who comes to kill, steal, and destroy. We also know the situations in which our weaknesses are most vulnerable, so we'll do our utmost to stay out of those situations if we have a short fuse or a confrontational nature. Most potential battles are best avoided.

Nothing Can Separate Us from the Love of God

I first encountered this desperately downcast person at various locations along the south coast of Tenerife. Tragically, due to her pitiful appearance – a tangled mass of unkempt hair, tattered clothing and hardened weather-beaten face. It was initially hard to figure out even what sex she was.

Everything about her screamed homeless and destitute, as I offered her little more than an inauspicious glance, although she responded aggressively to being approached.

Eventually, it dawned on me that not all that long ago this woman was just a little girl, someone's child, and that now she could be someone's mother, sister, or grandmother. But even in her sad, desperate state she was a Child of God and precious to Him.

We, too, are often forlorn souls who find it hard to accept God's love, to surrender to it, or even to believe in it at all. Some of us were raised in homes in which we were denied tactile love; that intimate, affectionate form of tenderness, so essential if a child is to grow into adulthood feeling wanted and cared for. This may be the case regardless of whether we were lavished with expensive gadgets or taken on foreign holidays.

Thankfully, our Lord understands the grim desolation of a loveless childhood. He mourns for the internal wilderness created by being starved of human love. Remarkably, He loves us just as we are, regardless of whether we accept Him or not. To love Him in return, however feebly, is the minimum He requires from us.

The Velveteen Rabbit by Margery Williams is a timeless story about a boy who loved a dishevelled toy rabbit so much it became real. Similarly, often by the time we humans become real, we too are losing our hair and falling to bits! This book becomes a wonderful metaphor for human life by showing us that unconditional, sacrificial love can break through the barriers we often erect to keep people out and forcing them to relate to our counterfeit self. When barriers come down through accepting God's love and grace, we too become real, capable of loving others and even ourselves.

As CS lewis finely puts it: "To love at all is to be vulnerable. Love anything and your heart will certainly be wrung and possibly broken. If you want to make sure of keeping it intact, you must give it to no one, not even to an animal". William Barclay, the famous Scottish author, also reminds us: "More people have been brought into the Church by the kindness of real Christian love than by all the theological arguments in the world".

The temptation is always there for us to withdraw into ourselves, to treasure the "self-life", to cocoon ourselves in egocentricity in which we stay safe from the hard knocks that inevitably come our way if we dare to love unconditionally.

It's effortless to love those who look good, smell good, and most importantly, make us look good! However, growing to love those who antagonise us, bore us, repulse us, ignore us, manipulate us, and continually criticise us, summons incredible grace and understanding.

Many of us men struggle with emotion. After all, it rubs against the machoism so ingrained in Scottish society. Showing vulnerability by expressing genuine compassion and affection is often considered unmanly. Yet, the shortest verse in the Bible is: "Jesus wept". (John 11:35)

So, let us ensure that like the Velveteen Rabbit we reach our twilight years, shedding genuine tears, truly accepting one another, and most of all, that we dare to love as Jesus Himself loved.

Love is Never a Reason to Tolerate Disrespect

We are worthy of respect in relationships, but we can get derailed, confused, and demoralised when our love, loyalty and affection are not reciprocated. It is then that we doubt ourselves, question our true value and often feel rejected and embittered. There can also be a tendency to drown in a sea of self-condemnation as we reflect on how we could have handled things better.

We are born in the Image of God, and we are worthy of respect – but not at any cost. When I was a young man, on more than one occasion my mother would say to me: "You've made your bed, so you better lie in it" when she could see I was stressed about a relationship. It was a statement that made perfect sense at the time, but this phrase indicates that we are powerless to recreate a better outcome and should therefore tolerate anything in a relationship.

While loyalty and commitment are vital in a relationship, tolerating disrespectful behaviour will stifle and smother it.

If we allow someone to constantly disrespect us, we inevitably start to disrespect ourselves. This becomes demoralising if we honour someone and we are not treated with anything like the same level of respect in return. Love is a strong emotion and can easily cloud our judgement.

By the grace of God, may all our relationships be mutually respectful.

The Power and Deep Contrition of Genuine Tears

In nearly all cultures and continents crying is associated with tears trickling down the cheeks, accompanied by characteristic sobbing sounds. But in our different cultures we also respond differently to the sight of someone crying.

Particularly Males can be ridiculed for crying and from an early age they may have been taught that they shouldn't cry. However, if boys and men aren't encouraged to cry, at least occasionally, even in private, fear, frustration, depression, and anger get suppressed and can amplify.

Crying can be viewed as a sign of weakness in a culture embedded in machoism.

Tears, those salty drops of liquid that spill from your eyes when we least expect it, speak a language of their own. They are the ink of the soul revealing our emotions. Tears flow like splashes of joy when a good laugh squeezes them from the corners of our eyes.

I have cried more in the last 12 months than in all the previous

20 years put together; not only because crying is recognised as one of the symptoms of MND, but also because I feel more sensitive to the pain of others.

Tears are our body's release valve for stress, sadness, grief, anxiety, and frustration. Also, we can have tears of joy, like when a child or grandchild is born, or tears of relief when a massive obstacle has been overcome. Tears can also be used to control; we can control with our words, as well as our tears.

Physically, tears express the pain we feel – a sudden sadness or an unspeakable agony. Tears can be liquid pain or liquid joy. They know no age limit; a new-born bairn announces its arrival by bawlin and greetin, and in a nursing home we may witness the tragic sight of an old dementia patient walking the corridors sobbing.

Tears have a way of making their appearance at family events such as weddings and funerals. In sport, many of us can recall the tears of snooker champion Alex Higgins at the crucible in 1982 and of football favourite Gazza at Italia 90, as we witnessed ecstasy for Higgins and agony for Gascoigne. For them, their heart was too close to their eyes, as the glare of the sporting world looked on.

The shortest verse of the Bible is "Jesus Wept". (John 11:35) It's not only the shortest verse but also one of the shortest lessons in Scripture – a lesson in compassion, loyalty, and love.

When we are full of sadness and tears are flowing there's no shame to do the jobs around the house with tears in our eyes. There's nothing wrong with conversing with our tears at our lowest ebb: Tears, I feel you. You make me want to quit life but there are family and friends to come along side me and dishes to be washed, my car to be sorted or a sermon to be written.

Our eyes do need a good wash with tears every now and then, so that we can see life with a clearer view again. The psalmist reminds us that he who goes out weeping, bearing the seed for sowing, shall come home with shouts of joy.

There is a sacredness in genuine tears; they are not the mark of weakness, but of power. They speak more eloquently than ten thousand tongues. They are the messengers of overwhelming grief, of deep contrition, and of unspeakable pain.

You are Fearfully and Wonderfully Made

If you are skinny, you must be anorexic. If you're overweight, you must be a glutton. If you smoke dope, you're a junkie. If you drink regularly, you are a drouth. If you dress up, you must fancy yourself, and if you dress down, you're gan aboot like a tink.

If you speak your mind, you are arrogant and confrontational. If you don't say anything or don't fit in with the crowd, you are snobbish. If you are sociable, you're accused of wanting to be the centre of attention. If you are reserved, you are standoffish and aloof.

If you live in a grand house, you are materialistic and are only trying to keep up with the Joneses. If you own an expensive car, that's a status symbol. If you get promotion at work, you are sucking up to the boss. If you are a Christian, you are a homophobic do-gooder.

If you are suffering from depression you need to stop feeling sorry for yourself and snap out of it. If your child goes off the rails, it's due to parental neglect. And if you are not very bright academically you are a gype!

We can't do much in this world without being criticised or

labelled. The truth is, we live in a culture where people get great satisfaction through judging the next person. And let's face it, none of us can claim to be the ultimate paragon of virtue in this respect. Our culture is very apt at pulling other people down, but we should be allowed to be who we are.

There's always space for us to celebrate each other's uniqueness and quirkiness. When we judge others, we don't really define them, we define ourselves.

Let's build each other up. We are all fighting an internal battle no one knows about. Never forget that you are fearfully and wonderfully made!

Kindness Tells a Hurting Soul They Really Matter

There is no such thing as a small act of kindness; every simple act creates a ripple in the heart of the most lost or hardened soul. If we ever feel led to rescue a day from the tentacles of boredom and dejection, do an overgenerous deed, a kindness without remuneration or agenda, a deed for which we cannot be repaid. And let us be kind to ourselves too. God thinks we're worth His kindness, and He is a good judge of character.

"Be kind to one another, tender-hearted, forgiving one another, as God in Christ forgave you". (Ephesians 4:32 ESV)

ALLOW JESUS TO UNTIE THE KNOTS IN YOUR LIFE

Did you have a hard time learning to tie your shoelaces? I certainly had! I have always struggled with knotting my tie too, but that's a story for another day! At the age of five, tying shoelaces by cleverly making a simple knot with two tidy loops was a massive personal challenge for me.

Who came up with the idea of shoes anyway? I used to sit at my desk in primary one and had to ask a classmate not only to tie my shoelaces, but also tell me which shoe went on which foot!

Initially, I would have a stab at tying my own laces but before long I would be frantically trying to disentangle great muckle knots. I would grow more anxious and frustrated by the second and eventually, with a greetin face and tear-filled eyes, I would turn to someone beside me and ask: "Can you untie knots and tie my shoelaces for me?"

Jesus loves that request! Life gets tangled for us, both as kids and in adulthood. We goof up. We get ourselves in a pickle. We will never outgrow the urge or need to look up and say: "Help me!" And when we do, look who shows up: Jesus, our next-door Saviour!

Ah, the knots of our life! Knots of discord in our family. The knots of deep hurts in relationships. The absence of peace and joy in the home. Knots of hurt and resentment that so torture our hearts. How they suffocate the soul, drag us down, betray the heart's joy, and can even take away the will to continue living.

May Jesus "The Untangler of life's knots" wrap you in His arms of love, keep you under His protection and enlighten you with His peace today. Go ahead and ask Him: "Do you untie knots?" Even if it's just a simple granny knot, ask Him to untangle the knots in your life.

He will never disappoint you.

Enthusiasm Makes All the Difference

Back in the 1980s, it would have been unlikely for me to have taken any interest in a televised dart match if it wasn't for the unparalleled enthusiasm of TV-commentator Sid Waddell. Sid was as much a part of the framework of the occasion as the smoke congested arena or the heart jumping amplified thump of a tungsten dart on the hemp board.

Only Murray Walker's boyish excited commentating voice, comparable in pitch and speed to the Formula 1 engines, and Bill McLarens infectious enthusiasm in rugby union came anywhere near to transcending his beloved sport in the same manner that Waddell could. They had the ability to make the mundane amazing.

This operates on the premise that attitude is the key to every passing moment. In our country it can be the case that when someone not familiar with this truth meets a real enthusiast, he or she may find them a bit OTT or even a bit "touched".

Several years ago, I went out with Julia, a lady from Edinburgh. I learned so much from Julia in terms of passion, enthusiasm, and positivity. I wasn't used to such enthusiasm in my life, and when I asked her the secret of her enthusiasm, she told me that she had learned to appreciate and focus her attention on living in the present. She added that most people spend their time either focusing on what went wrong in the past or worrying about the future.

I was then able to see that enthusiasm had the ability to take what many of us would gloss over and inject it daily with fresh vigour and passion. Genuine enthusiasm is infectious and can spread like wildfire if our hearts are open to its passion. Often our problems have nothing to do with our job, relationships, or bank balance: The real problem lies deep within us.

When we are born, Almighty God builds enthusiasm into our being. As we emerge from infancy to childhood, we are filled with excitement at the awe-inspiring wonder of life. Everything is new and fascinating. But as we grow older, we can become too sophisticated and cynical as our world view begins to harden, and sadly, we can then lose one of the most precious virtues of human nature: enthusiasm.

The problem of sustaining enthusiasm can become increasingly difficult because the natural enthusiasm of our youth starts to take a fearful battering as the years begin to add up. Countless disappointments, rejections, dashed hopes and ambitions all conspire to drain our energy which in turn dims enthusiasm.

The word enthusiasm comes from the Greek "en theos" literally meaning: "God within". This explains why Nihilism – the belief that there is nothing – inevitably leads to depression and despair. This may go some way to explain why someone who commits to following Jesus in many cases discovers an inner explosion of joy and enthusiasm. Do we ever whistle while we work with a broad smile when washing the dishes or mowing the grass?

Let us allow enthusiasm to help uplift our world. After all, if we are on this journey together, we might as well appreciate the view, rather than scurry morbidly to our chosen destination whining and complaining as we go along.

Ultimately, enthusiasm is not only generated by good things that happen to us, but also the realisation that we are all part of that good thing called life, which can have genuine meaning and expectancy.

THE REMARKABLE VICAR OF BAGHDAD

Among the many diverse and fascinating servants of the Lord my good friend, the late John Coppard and I had the privilege to interview for our "Coffee with Pastors" online outreach, was Cannon Andrew White – more commonly known as The Vicar of Bagdad.

I had been a long-time admirer of Cannon Andrew's remarkable ministry that has borne incredible fruit over the years in the most challenging of circumstances. Canon Andrew White is a remarkable man of God. Often referred to affectionately as The Vicar of Baghdad, he is one of the few people trusted by virtually every side in the complex Middle East conflict.

At age thirty-two, he was diagnosed with multiple sclerosis, a disease that has affected his speech and left him bedridden. It's obvious that his own suffering has made him more sensitive to the suffering of others. During the time he led St George's Church, the only Anglican Church in Iraq in the heart of Baghdad's Red Zone, it was targeted and damaged by countless bombs.

Andrew White is clearly not too enamoured by theory, nor is he sympathetic towards legalistic religion that attempts to take a one-dimensional approach to interfaith dialogue. Unlike many stereotypical and judgemental people of all faiths, he respects and honours the faith and commitments of leaders of other religious groups – Jewish, Muslim, and others, so there can be a transparent exchange and an honest approach to the issues of underlying conflicts.

Cannon White was once summoned to a late evening dinner with Uday and Qusay Hussein, the infamous sons of Saddam Hussein, and he works closely with both Sunni and Shia Muslims in Iraq. He has also broken bread with Yasser Arafat and been involved in intense dialogue with Hamas and Israeli leaders.

Iraq's Christians have fled by the hundreds of thousands in recent years, as families have been persecuted by Islamic Extremists. Out of around 1.5 million in 2003, only about 200,000 remain. This is especially tragic, as the Christian communities in Iraq are ancient and indigenous. They are not post-colonial, nor have they been established by Western missionaries. In fact, Iraq's Christian community is one of the oldest in the world, dating back to the first century. An early tradition says it was founded by Thomas, "Doubting Thomas", one of the 12 disciples.

Many churches still speak Aramaic, the language of Jesus.

Canon Andrew White's remarkable ministry has come with a price; not the least of which is his transcontinental commuter marriage. His wife and children still reside in England, and he tries to get home to see them for several days each month.

Back in the Middle East, by necessity, he wears a bullet proof jacket over his clerical collar, with a large silver cross gracing his chest. He is in and out of helicopters and war zones with the briskness of a gospel-toting Bruce Willis. Canon White is endowed with a remarkable ability to face mortal danger and remain fearless. He concedes that he hears Jesus saying to him: "Don't take care. Take risks".

During his time in Iraq, he admitted with typical frankness: "I live with a price on my head. The kind of people that I spend my time engaging with are not usually very nice. On the whole nice people do not cause wars". He is undoubtedly a man of backbone, not wishbone. The Iraqi government eventually acknowledged his worth as a reconciliatory figure in what remains a powder-keg political and religious situation. During this time, he had as many as 35 armed guards, many of them Muslims, on a rota for his protection.

One Sunday, on his way to lead a service at Church, Canon White counted sixty dead bodies strung up on lampposts and discarded along the road – victims of all the latest round of post-invasion sectarian violence. Earlier this year, speaking in Jerusalem, he lamented that 1,096 of his own parishioners had been killed over only a five-year period.

Yet, despite these horrific statistics, St. George's continued to provide food and clothing for the surrounding area, and it maintains a clinic offering free medical and dental help. And under Canon Andrew's ministry the attendance numbers in Church never diminished.

Incredibly, several hundred Muslim women worshipped there too.

Now bedridden due to the ravages of MS, Cannon Andrew White is without doubt the most glaringly deserving recipient of the Nobel Peace Prize we will ever come across. But with the servant heart of his Lord and Saviour, his only desire is to witness peace and reconciliation in Iraq and the Middle East.

Fruitfulness in Old Age

A striking and encouraging fact of life in an often-gloomy culture is that people are generally living longer due to the expertise and advancements in modern medicine that are helping to prolong human life. With this is mind, it's worth remembering that some of the most precious words in Scripture are to do with old age, and some of the most cherished and hopeful promises are given to the elderly.

The writer of Proverbs reminds us: "The glory of young men is their strength, but the beauty of old men is in their wisdom". Job touches on the same idea when he says: "Wisdom is with the aged and understanding in length of days".

This does not necessarily mean that foolishness is never found in the old and wisdom cannot be found on young shoulders. After all, I am approaching the age of sixty and am still prone to moments of madness and foolishness! However, better a mature eighteen-year-old than someone treble or quadruple that age who has refused to grow up!

History has shown that there have been many old fools, as well as youthful sages. But Scripture suggests that, on balance, the elderly who have had the willingness and humility to learn great grace and wisdom in the hard school of life are to be offered due respect and honour.

Beware of People Who Brag

We Westerners love superlatives and horn blowing. Or perhaps boasting and horn blowing transcends all nations and is more widespread than I imagine?

The phrases: "Biggest in the world", "Best in the world", "A cut above the rest", "This is my gifting" are on many a lip. If we are called, if we are anointed, if we are gifted it will be self-evident. There is never a need to brag.

As Spurgeon once said: "You will never exaggerate when you speak good things of God. It is not possible to do so. Try, dear brethren, and boast in the Lord".

Walk with the Broken – Don't Sit with the Great

As bairns we may have had dreams of rubbing shoulders alongside the lofty and the famous, but some of us carry this craving into adulthood – even in Christian ministry. As a new Christian, I remember being so excited about speaking briefly to Nicky Cruz at a testimony night in Fraserburgh but then, working in the Broch a few weeks later, totally ignoring a drug addict in a shop doorway.

Do we still have a craving to sit alongside the big hitters or the big names? Or to be seen in the company of those who look good, smell good, and help make us look good.

There are many humble, compassionate followers of Christ, but there remains an element of haughtiness in the Christian Church. To be haughty is to regard ourselves better than others, to look down on other people because we feel superior in our intellect, in our lifestyle, or our achievements.

In sharp contrast, Jesus Christ is the epitome of humility; the Eternal Love humbling itself, clothing itself in the garb of meekness and gentleness, to win and serve and save us.

This is a timely reminder for many of us and gives a fresh

perspective of how Christ walked on this earth. He sat with the broken, the marginalised and oppressed. He walked alongside them, healed them, and set them free. When asked why He did this, He said that the broken were the reason His Father had sent Him to earth.

The seemingly great and lofty often feel they don't need healing, but we all carry an element of brokenness and insecurity. No one is infallible.

The broken realise they are broken; they have no pretence.

Seek First the Kingdom of God

Seek first the Kingdom of economic wealth and we will worry about every penny and every pound. Seek first the Kingdom of perfect health and we will worry about every bump and blemish.

Seek first the Kingdom of popularity and we will obsess about every conflict or disagreement and judge our worth by the amount of "likes" we get on Facebook.

> Seek first the Kingdom of thrills and excitement and we will always crave a bigger hit or a bigger buzz.
> Seek first the kingdom of social status and that dream house or that new car will never truly satisfy.
> Seek first the Kingdom of position or recognition and we will always be frustrated or feel overlooked.
> Seek first the Kingdom of safety and we will never take a risk and abdicate our God-given purpose and destiny.

But seek First the Kingdom of God and we will find it.

Seek first His Kingdom, above all else, and He will grant us all we need and more.

Time to Reignite the Dreamer Within You

Empathetic people – dreamers & idealists – appear to have this sort of accidental power. Most of them spend their early years riddled with self-doubt, insecurity, and with people pleasing habits. Often, they find themselves oppressed in controlling narcissistic relationships where their journey is inevitably derailed when this comfortable life gets uprooted by an unexpected darkness.

Suddenly their trusted methods no longer seem to bring them happiness and they become shrouded in self-doubt, whereby all innocence and confidence is drained from them. At first, this depression convinces them that they might never feel joyful again, but ultimately, it sets them on a quest for something more: love, compassion, justice, and wisdom. Once this adventure begins, there is no stopping a dreamer.

And when dreamers unite? Well, that's how we start to change the world.

ANGER – A DANGEROUS EMOTION

Many of us remember Bjorn Borg as the ice-cool Swede who rarely showed any emotion on the tennis court; someone who never became angry at the linesmen or the umpire. But Borg's self-control was learned and developed – he didn't receive that at birth. Apparently, when a youngster, Borg displayed an on-court temper, similar to that of his great adversary, John McEnroe. He was also prone to swearing and throwing rackets.

At the age of 13 he was suspended by his tennis club for six months. His parents supported that expulsion by locking up his racket and refusing to let him play. Borg now says that he learnt his lesson and from that day onwards simply decided to control his temper – and he certainly did that.

When I was younger, I too was a bit of a hothead. Having red hair was a convenient excuse for my quick temper that was often borne out of impatience or a grandiose sense of injustice. Eventually, it dawned on me that acting angrily to a situation made it impossible to understand other people's perspectives. I also realised that unjustified anger only oversimplifies, amplifies, and magnifies the negative aspect of an issue and often blows it out of proportion.

Anger is one of the most powerful and complex of emotions. It can be either the catalyst that enables us to achieve the seemingly impossible or the stumbling block that snares us in a lifestyle dominated by bitterness, broken relationships, gracelessness and even violence.

Eugene Peterson, the author of *The Message Bible*, says: "Anger is a legitimate emotion. It isn't a sin any more than laughter is. All the same, anger is a dangerous emotion. It can easily consume us, and in consuming us lead to our condemnation".

To quote Aristotle: "Anyone can become angry. That is easy. But to be angry with the right person, to the right degree, at the right time, for the right purpose and in the right way . . . that is not easy".

Frustration is often the catalyst for angry feelings and behaviour. We can feel a certain amount of frustration whenever something or someone thwarts our progress. However, most anger we feel about our current circumstances is often rooted in our past.

Rejection and anger go hand in hand, and very few of us have grown up rejection-free. Might it be that the unresolved issues of the past feed our anger? In Ephesians 4:26, Paul tells us to let the sun go down on our anger, but we often struggle to do so.

The classic song *In the Ghetto* (originally titled *The Vicious Circle)* was made famous by Elvis Presley in 1969. It's a stark reminder of generational poverty with a central theme of anger running through it. It's about a child born in a Chicago ghetto to a mother who already has more children than she can feed. He soon learns how to steal and fight. He grows up to be an angry young man.

Then, one day, he purchases a gun and steals a car. He attempts to run but is shot and killed, just as his own son is born. The strong implication is that the new-born's fate will be the same as his father's, and that the seemingly unescapable vicious circle of anger, frustration and hopelessness will remain unbroken. The reality is that despite our life circumstances we did not come into this world as hotheads and thankfully we don't have to depart from it as hotheads either.

Ellel Ministries have what is affectionately called an "anger tree", a redwood tree with soft bark where someone with pent-up anger can punch the trunk without damaging either their hand or the tree. Others are encouraged to release their anger by skimming stones across the surface of a pond or lake or throwing pebbles into the sea. The ministry team even encourage clients to punch pillows, pound mattresses and beat the cushions of an armchair to release pent-up anger.

God wants us to forgive those who have hurt or upset us. This is far from easy, but as Paul reminds us in Colossians (3;13) 2: "Bear with each other and forgive whatever grievances you may have against one another. Forgive as the Lord forgave you".

Finding Joy in the Journey

As I grow older I slowly and stubbornly learn never to regret a day of my life because I appreciate that too many good people never make it to the age I am now.

This old hymn reminds us: "Count your blessings, name them one by one. And it will surprise you what the Lord has done".

Good, productive days are most welcome, even in a body that's being ravaged by MND. They are by far our preferred option, although bad days when everything seems to go pear-shaped simply give us life experience to learn from and hopefully something others will be able to relate to in their hour of need. Both are essential for a balanced, meaningful life.

In a sense, we are just as happy as we make our mind up to be, regardless of our circumstances. We crave happiness but happiness is an external feeling and always self-gratifying, while true joy stays with us.

True joy gives us inner peace, while true happiness is often fleeting. However, some people believe they'll only be happy and content if they go and live somewhere else or be with someone else.

It can be very tempting to look for pastures new when we are emotionally fragile, but it seldom works out that way, unless we are clearly led there by God. Wherever we go, we inevitably take our unresolved issues with us.

There is no bell curve of joy like there is of happiness. Eventually, we'll stop laughing. Even hyenas stop laughing.

Joy sustains our reactions and fleeting feelings. Simply put: Biblical joy is choosing to respond to external circumstances with inner contentment and satisfaction, because we know that God will use these experiences to accomplish His work in and through our lives, however grim or daunting that may seem on the outside.

Anxiety thrives in the cell culture dish of "if only". It doesn't survive in the world of "it's done". For that reason, a grateful word needs to follow each anxious thought. Ask God: "Lord, what is separating me from joy?"

Ask Him to replace your anxiety and worry with courageous joy.

Ask Him to help you anchor to the firm rock on His shoreline.

Ask him to show you the joy that cannot be stolen from you and He will oblige.

He will stir a revival of contagious joy in your heart this very day.

FINANCIALLY DESTITUTE, YET RICH IN SPIRIT

Some of the most joyful, loving, contented people I have met in my life had very little or no money to their name. They were financially destitute but rich in spirit. On the other hand, we hear this from Creflo Dollar: "Well, you need to hear about money, because you ain't gonna have no love and joy and peace until you get some money!"

What utter nonsense! God wants to prosper us in all areas of our life, not just in finance. In fact, the most financially fruitful period of my life was before I gave my life to Christ, and I believe I have been prospered in other areas of my life since then too.

There is nothing wrong with being financially comfortable, or even wealthy. In fact, some of the most gracious, humble, unassuming, and generous people I have come across have been financially independent. But if accumulating money or material wealth is our primary focus in life or the central point of our ministry, I would argue whether we will ever be truly joyful, loving, or live a peaceful and fulfilling life.

Humour Helps Us through Our Toughest Times

I am sure I was not alone in feeling deep sadness when hearing of the recent death of Doddie Weir. Although Doddie's final years were dominated by MND, at his funeral his sons explained how the disease was rarely talked about in the family, and that it never stunted the 61-cap Scotland second-row's famous sense of humour. He was so much more than just a retired former rugby union player; he was the slapstick clown of the dressing room, the pub, and the home – even when he had to a rely less on words, and had cruelly lost physical dexterity to gain his laughs and chuckles.

While there is nothing amusing about the cruel humour most of us encounter every day, kindly humour can be a powerful tool in the service of truth and much needed reforms, as this 21st century parody would indicate: "Humpty Dumpty sat on the wall. But so Humpty Dumpty wouldn't fall, he was sent by the head of human resource on a three week health and safety course".

Sarcasm, or "the lowest form of wit" as it is commonly termed, is only an unfortunate camouflage for insecurity and lack of confidence. Wisecracking may be funny at times, but one-upmanship is belittling and emotionally draining.

Former French president, Charles de Gaulle once threatened a Parisian cartoonist with imprisonment after he continually portrayed him as a clown. While I am sure that some British politicians would have welcomed the publicity resulting from appearing on Spitting Image, I can imagine that others would have been angered when some upstart script writer or producer exaggerated their facial features and idiosyncrasies to make them the butt of ridicule for millions of TV viewers.

Some may argue that there is a fine line between humour and blasphemy. We recall the controversial Danish cartoons, depicting Islamic prophet Muhammad as a suicide bomber, sparking a storm of Muslim protest several years ago. Similarly, many Christians did not see humour in how Christ's crucifixion was depicted in the controversial 1970s Monty Python film *The Life of Brian.*

Like power without humour, faith without humour may become a faith of arrogance and intolerance. Some of the most intolerant, fanatical, humourless people in our society tend to masquerade as Christians, Jews, Muslims, Humanists and Atheists who are convinced that they alone are right. This arrogance can also seep through to different denominations of the Christian faith who are just as convinced that their theology, doctrine, and style of worship is superior to others. Surely a sense of humour and the ability to laugh at ourselves can protect us from such delusions concerning our own righteousness and superior virtues?

James Thurber, the famous American wit and humorist once wrote: "Humour is counterbalance. Laughter need not be cut out of anything since it improves everything. The power, that created the poodle, the platypus, and people, has an integrated sense of both comedy and tragedy".

Many great world leaders are rarely comedians, although Volodymyr Zelensky, the Ukranian president was formerly an actor and comedian. Being able to see the funny side is often what enables well rounded people to overcome the trials and tribulations of life. Overtly religious people can tend to be intensely serious and often too holier-than-thou to have a laugh. The Pharisees who routinely confronted Jesus were such individuals, yet those who choose to walk with Christ in an authentic way are more likely to smile and not take themselves too seriously.

Jesus Himself was no stand-up comedian and the Gospel writers did not use "lol" or funny face emoticons to describe His ministry. The Gospels are punctuated with crowds rejoicing in good spirits and with laughter, culminating in Jesus' final entrance into Jerusalem. Such events could only have been incredibly exciting.

Remember: Jesus' preaching of the "Beatitudes" directs people to be happy and blessed in a world distorted by sickness, poverty and evil.

In Days Gone By

In days gone by, the Church bells wid ring and l knew it wis time to surface from the land of nod and the excesses o the night afore and get masel riggit for the pub.

I wid tak ma customary Sunday morning jaunt from ma hoose doon the doctor's laney, past the Kirk, wi my usual thumping hangover on my y ti the Park Hotel. This is exactly what I believed!

That the al' grey ootdated church wis where perfect, goody-goody, dressed up saddos wid go. But, instead, I wis ti find at nithing could be further fae the truth: Wi' open arms, the church welcomed waifs, strays and misfit's like me. In fact, the church is nae a prehistoric lecture theatre for saints, it's a hospital for sinners who realise they dinna hae it a together.

Never Write Off the Small Rural Church

We can sometimes be tempted to dismiss the wee rural or parish Church in all its smallness, its apparent drabness and perceived non-excitedness. Those places of worship that have struggled numerically and financially for years, even decades, with a handful of loyal servants despite the many prophecies and predictions of their demise.

We may serve or lead in an area or a parish with the richest soil, where every seed planted appears to spring to life; where the seasons are kind, the vegetation is lush, the harvest plentiful. But some places are merely stony ground, and faithful mission and ministry in that field might be picking out the wee stones between the golden barley for several generations.

The question the parable throws back at the Church is: What kind of growth can we expect from the ground and conditions we work with? This is why the current unilateral emphasis and obsession on numerical Church growth can be so demoralising and disabling.

But God is faithful.

Praise God for the mega Church and for any model of Church.

But having watched the rise and fall of Mars Hill Church and the scandal hit Hillsong documentaries I am not remotely surprised that the wee local Church dogmatically seems to outlive many impressive, slick new movements that are housed in state-of-the art buildings, full of personality preachers and superstar worship teams. Those business modelled empires have gone up and come down again like a spectacular eight-minute fireworks display at Hogmanay.

Floating through life as a casual agnostic for many years, I confess to not having had a very flattering view of anyone who professed their Christian faith. I could never properly discern whether they deserved my pity or ridicule. Subsequently, when I did come to faith, I realised it would be somewhat hypocritical if I took umbrage to others who viewed me in the same manner!

Since becoming one of them, I can only conclude that without doubt Christians are indeed oddities. However, it's reassuring to know that we are in good company. In Mark chapter 3 a crowd said that Jesus was out of his mind (verse21) and possessed (verse22). In John chapter 10, they said Jesus was demon possessed and raving mad. Consequently, it's no surprise that they treated His disciples with the same contempt. For example, after Paul gave his testimony to King Agrippa, he was accused of being out of his mind. (Acts 26:24)

Such thoughts were not limited to the fanatics of the First Century.

There is No Perfect Church, Only a Perfect God

I was raking through some old emails and came across my first ever Christian article written in the Portsoy Church of Scotland magazine called "Focus" in July 2006.

I feel that people may visit churches because they are searching for something different. Many have an understanding that the Church is a place of help and spiritual guidance. They may have a shallow belief in God but don't realise that Jesus is the key to the Christian faith. They are experiencing a spiritual void in their life. This is a void that we attempt to fill with just about everything imaginable, from alcohol to adventurism.

Many come with hurts and worries. What they seek is a touch from God that will change their lives forever. When this does not happen, they'll feel let down, disappointed and disillusioned. Some may not relate to the style of worship, the preacher's sermon or they feel unwelcome. They may only attend Church once or twice and not come back but leave with their Church experience having been a negative one.

How different things might have been if they had met someone they could have related to – a listener, an empathiser; someone who could have told them that Christianity is not about a building, a set of rules, or hard to sing hymns and songs with words that can be difficult to understand.

However, despite its failures and blunders throughout centuries, the Church is still the avenue God chooses to nourish us. I guess it all boils down to what someone told me as a new Christian: "When you find the perfect Church don't join it – you'll spoil it!" Christianity is about child-like faith, not child-like thinking.

Followers of Christ cast off the shackles of a Godless society of sceptics and intellectual experts. Some people define it as an optimistic philosophy of life. Many regard it as a set of morals to live by, or something that gives you a good feeling about yourself or gives you an incentive to do good things. Still others dismiss it as something for the intellectually weak.

Christianity is none of these. To put it simply: Christianity is a relationship, a way of life based upon the example, teachings and miracles of Jesus Christ. Christianity is not a list of things for us to do, but rather our only true hope, for it tells what Jesus came to do for us all.

CHRISTIANS ARE ODDBALLS!

Just casually browse through the history of the Christian Church and you would see countless individuals who have been considered unbalanced because of their allegiance to Christ. For example, those who gave their lives as martyrs, stood in public places to speak passionately of Christ, and those who rejected prestigious and lucrative careers to humbly serve their Saviour in some remote part of the world.

No wonder AZ Tozer wrote: "A real Christian is an odd number anyway. He feels supreme love for one whom he has never seen, talks familiarly every day to someone he cannot see, expects to go to heaven on the virtue of another, empties himself in order to be full, admits he is wrong so he can be declared right, goes down in order to get up, is strongest when he is weakest, richest when he is poorest, and happiest when he feels the worst. He dies so he can live, forsakes in order to have, gives away so he can keep, sees the invisible, hears the inaudible, and knows that which passes knowledge".

The Bible is littered with oddballs and none more so than John the Baptist. Matthew wrote: "John's clothes were made of camel's hair, and he had a leather belt around his waist. His culinary habits were quite simple too. He lived on a smorgasbord of locusts and wild honey". (Matthew 3:4)

The Old Testament prophet Isaiah was someone else who didn't shop at the Hebrew version of NEXT or splash on some Aramaic aftershave when we read in 2 Kings 1:8: "They replied, He had a garment of hair, with a wide leather belt".

If our Christian faith might cause the loss of some friends, the approval of our family, or the mockery of our workmates, often the tendency is to travel the path of least resistance. In truth, genuine friends will never desert us regardless of what we believe. While the blight of exclusive Religion through control and ostracism have been wreaking havoc in families and communities along this coast for many decades, modern times appear to have ushered in the neo-Christian anything goes believer.

As a result, it's easy to become embarrassed or ashamed of the gospel of Christ. (Romans. 1:16) Indeed, some of us may be reluctant to admit it or even recognise it, as evidenced by our non-committal and apathetic attitude. It is sometimes called "chameleon religion", as we inadvertently fall into what might be termed "Laodicean lethargy". We then become more concerned about protecting our image, due to the fear of what others think or say, rather than following the example of Christ.

In *Mere Christianity*, C S Lewis writes of Jesus: "You must make your choice. Either this man was, and is, the Son of God, or else a madman or something worse. You can shut him up for a fool, you can spit at him and kill him as a demon, or you can fall at his feet and call him Lord and God but let us not come with any patronising nonsense about his being a great human teacher. He has not left that open to us. He did not intend to. Now it seems to me obvious that He was neither a lunatic nor a fiend: and consequently, however strange, or terrifying, or unlikely it may seem, I have to accept the view that He was and is God".

So, the next time someone belittles you for being "sad" or "deluded" because you choose to follow Jesus Christ – rejoice! Be encouraged: You are in the best of company!

When Jesus says in Matthew 10:31: "You are worth more than

many sparrows", you can trust Him. He knows the value of every creature.

And when Jesus says: "In my Father's house are many mansions", you can count on it. He knows: He has walked through them.

Too often we crave validation from others and for our achievements and yes, it's great to accomplish and be recognised, but our true worth and our true identity is in Christ.

CHARISMANIA VS
CHARISPHOBIA

As a charismatic I believe that the spiritual gifts of 1st Corinthians chapter 14 are very much for today. In fact, Scotland has a powerful prophetic history. Many of the great 16th century reformers were prophets of God and we witnessed the fruit of prophesy during the Lewis revival.

However, I am fully aware of the excesses of the charismatic movement, particularly regarding health, wealth, and prophesy. Unfortunately, terms like charismania and charisphobia are used to describe the extreme views and practices of the charismatic movement.

Charismania is seen as an often weird and whacky fleshly endeavour to imitate charisma. Where the most hyper frenzied of charismatics practically need scraped off the ceiling it's not difficult to see where the term originates from. We love mountaintop experiences, but we must also appreciate the less spectacular rhythms of Christian ministry. Charismania is simply any over-zealous human effort to do the work of the Spirit in the energy or ability of the flesh. Displays of charismania take on many forms and always draw attention to the persons themselves, rather than to Jesus.

On the other hand, the charisphobia rise appears to be an ultra cessationist stance that would go as far as claim that Pentecostals are heretics or demon possessed. I would suggest that if the likes of John McArthur and Justin Peters are genuinely led to speak out about the excesses of the charismatic movement they should do so in the spirit of love and grace, not through condemnation and judgement.

They focus on the extremes of the charismatic movement and conveniently overlook the vast majority of believers who believe in the gifts today, who remain rational and lucid.

We should avoid both Charismania and Charisphobia. In my view, we need Reformed and Pentecostal values such as mission, community outreach, evangelism, and care for the poor for the advancement of the Kingdom fuelled by the Holy Spirit.

Perfect Deceivers of
Our Worth

Have you ever considered that every job or deed from a pure heart is ultimately of equal value in the eyes of God? The nurse who gently injects the syringe, the scaffy who empties the bins, the farmer who ploughs the field, the postie who delivers the mail, the writer who guides the pen – all are of equal value in God's eyes. Monetary income and public adulation are the perfect deceivers of man's true worth.

I recall, on a decorating job, a lady I was working for being shocked that someone she knew had left his wife for another woman because he had a big job. I believe the gentleman she mentioned was an airline pilot. I wasn't a Christian at the time, but I was a bit perplexed that the lady concerned, a regular churchgoer, equated social status with human character.

Jesus sees us with the eyes of a Father – not the eyes of the world. He sees our defects, errors, blemishes, and our insecurities. He is enamoured by what we are doing when no one is watching, and no one is applauding. He sees our value.

What did Jesus know that enabled Him to do what He did? Here is part of the answer: He knew the value of people. He knew the value of you and me. He knew that each human being is special, made in His image. And because He did, we are not a source of stress to Him, we are a source of joy. Make sure you don't start seeing yourself through the eyes of those who don't value you.

When we know our true worth, no one can make us feel worthless. Never forget this promise: "For God so loved the world that he gave his one and only Son that whoever believes in him shall not perish. (John 3:16)

To love someone is to appreciate their true worth and to remind them of it if they have forgotten it. When Jesus speaks about His Father, He is the ultimate authority. Trust Him!

Reconciliation is a Beautiful Thing

Never tire of praying for reconciliation, as there are always fractured relationships within the Kingdom of God. Empathy and bucket-loads of grace are the first step towards genuine reconciliation. So is showing impartiality, in most cases, and refusing to play devil's advocate. R. Kent Hughes reminds us that the Cross is the ultimate evidence that there is no length the love of God will refuse to go in effecting reconciliation.

We make mistakes and we say and do things out of character. Even with honourable intentions we can be foolish, stubborn, and dogmatic, but never necessarily lacking in integrity or pure motive. What the enemy creates for bad, God eventually makes good, ending with beautiful reconciliation and restoration. God, in His mercy, never ends anything on a negative; all things done for the glory of God always ends on a positive for the Kingdom.

Bear with each other and forgive whatever grievances you may have one against another. Forgive as the Lord forgave you. (Colossians 3:13)

Idols, the Irresistable Gods of Our Age

We can laugh at people who lived thousands of years ago and worshipped idols – wood and stone gods – but the modern manifestations of idolatry are no less absurd and just as harmful to our well-being. Although we live in a secular culture, idols are still the irresistible gods of our age. With the global economy in a shambles, many of the idols we have worshipped for decades have tumbled down around us. Although most surface idols are enjoyable, harmless, and safe things, even if we treat them appropriately, we can so easily become too preoccupied, proud, or obsessed by them.

But deeper idols lurk more menacingly under the surface. They come in the form of security, significance, power, approval, and control. They are less tangible and often more difficult to detect. Any culture in which God is ignored, sex, money and political advancement become the unholy grail of many people. After all, Bob Dylan once sang: "You gotta serve somebody".

In his book *Counterfeit Gods* Timothy Keller writes: "Making an idol out of doctrinal accuracy, ministry success, or moral rectitude leads to constant internal conflict, arrogance and self-righteousness, and oppression of those whose views differ".

Our technocratic age offers remarkable technological advances and devotion to live internet streaming for power point business presentations, as well as Church sermons. When Churches put more emphasis on technology and technique rather than the Lord, these things also become idols. Church leaders can find themselves in the limelight of congregational idolatry. Although most can humbly accept praise and pass on the glory to God, others – like King Nebuchadnezzar in the Old Testament book of Daniel – may start to believe they are divine.

There is also an idolatrous "celebrity preacher" culture in the body of Christ today. There are believers who travel all over the country attending conferences of well-known preachers. Often, when they meet these preachers in person, they fawn over them and almost faint as they practically beg for selfies with them. Some huge churches and high-profile ministries have literally closed when their celebrity preacher stepped down – either voluntarily or in shame.

I first felt the pain of idolatry as a 9-year-old when Colin Stein, the centre forward I worshipped, was transferred from my beloved Rangers to Coventry City. I can vividly recall being in the depths of despair for days!

Next, I joined the ranks of millions of young men who were infatuated by1970s screen goddess Raquel Welch, who was to me the epitome of beauty and physical perfection. However, she later wrote in her memoirs: "I had acquired everything I wanted, yet I was totally miserable. I thought it peculiar that I had everything I wanted as a child – wealth, fame, and accomplishment in my career. I found it frightening that one could acquire all these things and still be so miserable".

Reinhold Niebuhr, a prominent 20th century theologian believed all humans struggle with a sense of being dependent and powerless. Rather than accept our vulnerabilities and dependency on a higher power, we desperately seek ways to assure ourselves of having complete power over our own lives. Neibuhr concluded that entire nations had corporate egos, just like individuals could have superiority and inferiority complexes.

Many Americans are unaware that on top of the most famous statue in the United States is the Roman counterfeit goddess, Libertas. Today, giant statues of Lenin and Stalin lie toppled in a Moscow sculpture park, as well as others around Tripoli and Baghdad – mute testimonies of oppressive counterfeit gods.

Whatever we have over-loved, idolised, and leaned upon in history, God over time has broken it and made us see the vanity of it as it comes tumbling down.

Even a commitment to control global warming can become all-obsessive, particularly in relation to other human needs, and our planet itself is viewed as god-like, rather than simply part of a created universe.

Is there any hope if our very souls are riddled with idols? Well, as Timothy Keller suggests: "The only way to free ourselves from the destructive influence of counterfeit gods is to turn back to the true one, the living God. He's the only one who, if you find him, can truly fulfil you, and if you fail him can truly forgive you".

THE SAD TALE OF BOB PIERCE

As a devotee to Christian humanitarianism, Bob Pierce succeeded in creating World Vision – one of the largest Christian relief organizations in the world. He travelled round America raising vast sums of money to build hospitals and orphanages. In 1959, at the height of his success, a journalist wrote: "Pierce cannot conceal his true emotions. He seems to me to be one of the few naturally, uncontrollably honest men I have ever met".

However, the same intensity also took its toll: Bob had an unbridled temper and frequently clashed with the World Vision Board, particularly over financial issues. He travelled much, for as many as 10 months of the year, and his family suffered. "I've made an agreement with God," he said, "that I'll take care of his helpless little lambs overseas if he'll take care of mine at home".

But it was all achieved at great cost as he continually neglected his family. It was during the rapid growth of World Vision that his wife and daughters were pushed further down Bob's priority list. When he did return home after ten months of travel, he was like a stranger in his own home, and naturally tension developed. Though he could sympathetically relate to a hurting world, his own family living under his own roof seemed so distant.

Later, one of his daughters committed suicide after he ignored her pleas to return home.

Pierce's relationship with his family suffered profoundly from his years abroad. In 1963, this saintlike legend, worn out by his constant travels, had a nervous breakdown. In 1967 he resigned from World Vision, feeling bitter towards those whom he felt interfered with his organization. Even though without Bob Pierce World Vision would not exist, his wife divorced him and eventually he died alone.

The story of Bob Pierce reminds me of passage from Susan Howatch's powerful novel *Glittering Images* – part of a six-book series set in the fictional town of Starbridge.

Writing about her experiences in the Church of England she tells us about a clergyman who devoted his life to always appearing godly, wise, loving, and charismatic: "Meanwhile his soul starves because no one knows him. They never meet the man I keep hidden. They just meet the man on public display. I call him the glittering image because he looks so good in the mirror. But beyond him lies an angry stranger who appears in the mirror whenever the glittering image goes absent without leave".

His ministry was his trophy, but also his prison.

I decided to share this tragic personal story because many of us will see a bit of Bob Pierce in ourselves. We can so easily get committed to what we perceive to be a wholesome cause, only to find ourselves gripped by service idolatry to such an extent that it encompasses every area of our lives.

Our own idol of high performance can be how we view practically anything. If we feel it's a bit substandard, lacking in bite or not very relevant for that time then the idol looks dismissively at us and once again we feel we have failed or under-performed. Most of us, at some point, have let ourselves become enslaved to the occasional idol. The idols of our own performance can easily take centre stage in our lives.

A friend of mine told me recently: "True service is about finding your pace. It's a marathon, not a sprint. As we pursue God, we must keep our lives in pace with His". (Galatians 5:25)

"Since we live by the Spirit, let us keep in step with the Spirit. Too fast is presumption, too slow and the cares and distractions of the world could overtake us."

The challenge is to find God's heartbeat and keep in step with His rhythm, not our own.

Howard Hughes – Wealth, Loneliness, Obsession and Fear

I became intrigued with the American billionaire Howard Hughes in the late 1970s, after hearing pop band *The Boomtown Rats* sing about his reclusive and eccentric behaviour.

It is said, that at one time Hughes was the richest man in the world. When his time on earth was nearing its end, Mr. Hughes went into a state of paranoia and began to keep himself locked up in a medical facility he had built for himself. In this building he went to the extent of trying to keep everything that came into contact with his person sanitised and clean of infectious germs that (in his mind) would surely end his life sooner than he wanted it to.

All his food, clothes, and toiletries were of a sanitised state, and those who brought him these things had to be sanitised too. He only had his hair cut and nails trimmed once a year. He had been in severe chronic pain from his extensive injuries, so much so that even the act of brushing his teeth was painful, so he avoided it.

He became obsessed with the 1968 film *Ice Station Zebra* and had it running on a continuous loop in his home. According to his aides he watched it at least 150 times.

Finally, Mr. Hughes had a special sanitation system installed equipped to keep germs from entering his body through the air he breathed. But in all his efforts to extend his life he still lived no longer than the average human. It was this bizarre lifestyle that was documented by *The Boomtown Rats* in the lyrics of "Me and Howard Hughes", as Bob Geldoff sang passionately:

"He's gonna lock himself up in his room.
Shutter the windows and bolt all the doors.
Wrap himself round in his Wall Street cocoon.
He's painting the ceiling, the walls, and the floor.
He's gonna lock himself up in his room.
And when he emerges have a new change of style.
He keeps saying things like it's me and Howard Hughes.
You'd wanna watch out for that dangerous smile".

In the divorce petition by his first wife, Ella, she called her husband irritable, cross, cruelly critical, and inconsiderate, rendering living together inappropriate.

Brown & Broeske, his biographers, commented: "Hughes always believed that problems with women could all be solved by externals: Fur coats, new houses, expensive cars, and showers of jewellery."

Despite all his money and all his lovers, Howard Hughes became increasingly lonely. Kathryn Grayson, one of his Hollywood lovers, said that Hughes seemed to be the loneliest man in the world.

Towards the end of his life, his inner circle was largely composed of Mormons – the only people he considered trustworthy – even though Hughes himself was not a member of their fellowship.

As I write about the life of Howard Hughes, I am reminded of the wise words of our Lord Jesus: "What does it profit a person to gain the whole world, yet lose their soul?" (Mark 8:36-37)

The Bible makes it clear that we will stand before our Creator one day. Jesus Himself says: "I tell you that on the day of judgment, people will give an account for every worthless word they speak." (Matthew 12:36)

Hughes has faced that judgement, rich as he was. He came into this world naked, and he left this world stripped of his family, his hopes, his dreams, his possessions, his worldly treasures, and finally his life.

When Mr. Hughes died in 1976, his possessions included 26 different companies, among which seven Las Vegas casinos, a struggling helicopter maker, several aircraft, a television station, private airport, regional airline, mining claims, and a bag of casino chips he neglected to redeem.

Who knows, Howard Hughes may have left this world unprepared for eternity. But during his lifetime he had everything one could ever want in this world: All the luxuries of the greatest of kings.

But his worldly gains would have amounted to very little in the end because in all his ventures to attain wealth and power he may well have left by the wayside the greatest eternal value of all: The Mercy and Atoning Blood of Jesus

Trust Takes Years
to Build and Seconds
to Break

Both would die on trees that day. One hung on a cross and the other swung from a branch. Their friendship spanned over three years. They ate together, laughed together, proclaimed the kingdom together, cast out demons together, battled with Pharisees together. The Servant King, stooping from His throne in Heaven, invited the man into His inner twelve. Night and day, this disciple did life with his Creator. Of course, we are speaking here of Jesus and Judas (Psalm 41:9)

Jesus would later lament: "Even my close friend in whom I trusted, who ate my bread, has lifted his heel against me".

We can bear the spiteful indignation of an enemy, but the quiet hatred of a false friend is something totally different. A false friend's dagger reaches deep into the recesses of our soul. Also, such flatterers know best where to strike, and Judas Iscariot knew where Jesus would be that fateful night.

"Follow me: I shall lead you to him," Judas grovelled.

Behold the glory and grace of this second man, a sinless man, who laid down His life for His friends. He conspired with His Father to undertake punishment in place of the criminal Barabas to save men of Judas' ilk.

See Him willingly betrayed, forsaken, oppressed; writhing under His Fathers wrath to redeem a cursed people from eternal judgment.

See Him embrace the thief on the cross to grant eternal life to the wicked but also the genuinely repentant thief alongside Him on the cross.

We are Stronger and More Resilient than We Think

What in nature created by God really wants to die? Everything struggles to live. Look at that tree growing in the shade, it gets hardly any sunlight and water only when it rains. It's growing out of dry infertile ground and it's strong because its hard life struggle is making it so.

We, too, can be strong that way. Life events may be horrible, shocking, or inescapable, but we always have a choice – not whether we can endure, but how we can endure, often against the odds, like the twisted, buckled tree that gets so little sunlight.

Legalism is Like a Hoose That's Nae a Hame

Legalism can be compared to a hoose that's nae a hame. What do I mean by that? Well, I once heard this analogy: Say, for instance, as a young loon or quine we visited a freens hoose for a few days. Everything looks good on the surface, food is plentiful, and It may have been an immaculately kept hoose with a bonnie weedless gairdin, but there was nae feeling of love there and no tangible warmth in the relationships.

Sadly, religious legalism focuses on perfect behaviour, while grace focuses on the blood of Christ.

All was based on appearance. In that seemingly tense environment, we were terrified to be oorsels because everything had to be perfect. Oor sheen always had to come aff at the front door, whether they were spotlessly clean or not, and we were even feart to ask to go for a pee! In short, it was a show house to impress, not a hame to bide in.

This is not to be confused with the countless Christ centred believers who simply like to have a nice comfortable, tidy home.

Likewise, legalism can produce a weel-intended religious person, but canna produce a true grace centred follower of

Christ. Legalism can only produce someone who goes through the motions of being Godly, striving always to look the part or portray infallibility. But legalism will never produce someone who is truly Christ centred because a hardened, critical, judgemental heart cannot also be one of love, humility, joy, grace, and peace.

Mothers Have a Special Place in Our Lives

My mother died 35 years ago, yet it often seems like only yesterday and rarely a day passes that I don't think about her, even fleetingly. You may well be fortunate enough to have your mother still with you, and I appreciate that you will have your own feelings and emotions when you reflect on her.

Perhaps your relationship with your mother is very close, or may be strained, but the maternal love and care she pours into your formative years and beyond can never be denied.

No one knows us better and worries about us like our mother and when she is gone the world seems a slightly different place with less security.

When your mother was in labour, she felt pain, but each time she gave birth she no longer focused on the anguish because of the joy that each baby brought to her. When your mother has passed away, you cannot turn to her anymore, and in a sense, it changes your life forever.

I sometimes think that I may have taken my mother for granted – and I'm sure we all feel that to a certain degree. There is no one created by God who knew us from the day we were born, who knew why we cried, or when we'd had enough food, who knew exactly what to say when we were struggling, and who encouraged us to live a good and honest life and taught us to treat people right.

Your mother always puts your happiness and well-being before her own. You could never do anything bad enough or wrong enough for her to stop loving you. But at the same time, we were never told as her cub: "Son, stay weak so the wolves can devour you". She always said: "Haud aff for yersel, clean that snot from your nose and stop yer greeting, this is the real world we are living in".

To be a mother is a call to suffering – not only at the beginning of life, but also throughout life and at the end. In the words of John Piper: "Wherever Christianity has become deeply rooted, the treatment of women has improved manifestly".

Jesus, however, added an even more personal touch, as He hung from nails in agony, staked to the cross. In the very midst of being publicly tortured to death, He still found time to honour His mother.

First, He saw her, and what unimagined horror did He witness on the face of His mother as she looked upon her crucified son? And not only did He behold her, but He gave His attention to her, and His words – in one of only seven recorded sayings from the cross – made provision for her after His death. And not just any provision, but He entrusted her to the disciple whom He loved.

Like Mary at Calvary, our mothers never have an agenda. They are far from flawless, but they are our mothers, regardless. When that layer goes, a good chunk of our childhood goes with her.

In summing up, the resilient mother knows that godly mothering is a by-product of the slow burn of commitment and faithfulness. She understands her resilience is not her claim on Christ, but the evidence of His claim on her.

A Father – Or a Dad

We have different thoughts and memories of our fathers, and they will be very much in our minds on Father's Day, their birthday, or, if your father is no longer with you, even on the anniversary of his passing.

Maybe your father was a fantastic father. Maybe he was absent, distant, aloof, or he abandoned you. But in any case, your father played his part in bringing you into this world. I have heard it said that a father should be his son's first hero, and his daughter's first love.

Billy Graham, the great 20th century evangelist said: "A good father is one of the most unsung, unpraised, unnoticed, and yet one of the most valuable assets in our society. Value you father".

In Proverbs 23:22 we read: "Listen to your father who gave you life, and do not despise your mother when she is old".

God bless all dads on Father's Day – stepdads, grandads, foster dads, single dads, soon to be dads, estranged dads, and the sadly no longer with us dads.

A father's tears and fears are often unseen, and his love often unexpressed. He is, or was, far from infallible, but his care and protection will always be a pillar of strength throughout your life.

And even when he is no longer with you, his example and his selfless sacrifice remain in your heart.

"Any man can be a Father, but it takes someone special to be a Dad". (Author Unknown)

THE VALUE OF TAKING
A DAY AT A TIME

Take a day at a time is almost a worn-out cliche but it is so true and simply profound. It is not about ignoring or sugar-coating the harsh realities we may be facing, but rather a sobering check for our often anxious and restless souls. More than 160,000 people around the world didn't wake up this morning and many of those would have been in good health with still much to live for.

Only now am I truly learning to appreciate the value of taking one day at a time. Looking back and yearning for the "normal" past can push us to an endless pit of melancholy, while looking too far ahead might be filled with many empty promises, leaving us in despair. At the same time, we should always live in hope and anticipation with dreams and aspirations. There is an equilibrium we tend to take for granted: The importance and blessing of the people who add value to our lives, and the small, seemingly insignificant things we do every day.

"One day at a time sweet Jesus
That's all that I'm asking from You.

Lord, give me the strength to do every day what I have to do.
Yesterday's gone, sweet Jesus, and tomorrow may never be mine.
Lord, help me today, show me the way, one day at a time".

SERVANT LEADERSHIP

According to Wikipedia, leadership has been described as "a process of social influence in which one person can enlist the aid and support of others in the accomplishment of a common task". It continues: "Studies of leadership have produced theories involving traits, situational interaction, function, behaviour, power, vision and values, charisma, and intelligence, among others. Somebody whom people follow; somebody who guides or directs others".

Different situations call for different leadership styles. Some rely primarily on personal charisma or intellect; some exude warmth and humility. Others exert power and authority, and still others resort to subtle manipulation and even enforcement.

From Moses to Mussolini and from King David to Winston Churchill, approaches to leadership run the gamut. Contexts differ, as do the leadership approaches that accommodate them.

Unlike conventional leadership approaches, using the top-down pyramid-shaped hierarchical style that we see in many business models, genuine servant leadership emphasises co-operation, trust, empathy, and the ethical use of potency.

At the heart of Jesus Christ's teaching is that every man is primarily a servant, making the conscious decision to lead, in order to better serve others – not to increase their own power. A true servant leader is concerned, not only about the present, but also about the next generation and will be mentoring and encouraging the next servant leader.

"But Jesus called them to Himself and said to them, "You know that those who are considered rulers over the Gentiles lord it over them, and their great ones exercise authority over them. Yet it shall not be so among you; but whoever desires to become great among you shall be your servant. And whoever of you desires to be first shall be slave of all. For even the Son of Man did not come to be served, but to serve, and to give His life a ransom for many." (Mark 10:42-45)

By His perfect example of servanthood, Jesus made it abundantly clear that He would not expect anything from us that He was not willing to do Himself. As God's only begotten Son He should have been served by His disciples, but instead He served them. Undoubtedly, service is the essence of Godly leadership.

The true servant leader's motivation, first and last, is service. Here, for instance, is what Mahatma Gandhi, perhaps the greatest example of servant leadership in the 20th century, said of his own motivation: "Service to the poor has been my heart's desire and it has always thrown me amongst the poor and enabled me to identify myself with them".

Servant Leadership is a difficult concept to wrestle with, as we have few modern-day examples to follow in a world obsessed by power and status.

The New Testament orientation of leadership was always organic, holistic, and functional – one that was based in the servant nature of Christ and grounded in God Himself, where there was freedom to edify, encourage, forgive, and bear one another's burdens while accepting each other's shortcomings and limitations. Elders, overseers, and shepherds were naturally appointed over time through example and character and foresight rather than through manipulation or coercion.

I recall being encouraged, while attending at a training event hosted by J John, an international Christian evangelist, as he shared that both he and his wife Killy were on the tea rota at the Church he pastors.

I was invited to a Go Global leaders' day out in Edinburgh, where walking up the Royal mile on our Christian Heritage tour was becoming more challenging for me due to the progression of MND that was hindering my walking.

As we entered one of the historical buildings, our lead pastor and founder, Pete Anderson instructed me to jump on his back, indicating he would carry me down a steep flight of stairs. I thought he was joking, as I am still more than13 stone in weight, but he was deadly serious. So, I got on to his back and he carried me down the stairs and back up again – remarkably, he never even broke sweat!

Jesus washing the feet of the disciples, just prior to His crucifixion, has incredible significance. (John 13:1-17) For Jesus, it was the display of His humility and His servanthood. For the disciples, the washing of their feet was in direct contrast to their carnal instincts at that time. Even Judas Iscariot, who left that table to betray the Lord, had his feet washed by Jesus. Remarkably, Jesus even put Himself in a position of servitude to His own betrayer.

You are the Greatest Miracle of All

The term "miracle" is used very broadly these days, particularly within the extremes of the Christian Church. We speak of miracle drugs, or of miracle babies and even miraculous comebacks in sport, but we often overlook the fact that we ourselves are a miracle.

Incredibly, we are the result of the fusion of one particular egg with one particular sperm. Apparently, each sperm, and each egg, is genetically unique because of the process of meiosis. A fertile woman has, on average, 100,000 viable eggs.

A man will produce about 12 trillion sperm over the course of his reproductive lifetime. So, let's say a third of those, 4 trillion are relevant to our calculation, since the sperm created after our mother hits the menopause don't count. That means the probability of that one sperm with half your name on it hitting that one egg with the other half of your name on it is an incredible one in 400 quadrillion!

David wrote in Psalms 139: "You knit me together in my mother's womb and I praise you because I am fearfully and wondrously made." You are a miracle regardless of how we view ourselves or are viewed by others. When we look in the mirror, at any age, we're looking at a miracle.

There has never been, nor will there ever be, anyone on this earth exactly like you or me. When we were born, the genius and divinity of God Almighty exploded into an original design and we were fearfully and wonderfully made. We are His divine masterpiece. In fact, if our personal genetic code was written out in longhand, it would be 3-billion letters long.

GIANNA SUVIVED HER OWN ABORTION

Gianna Jessen's mother was 17, and seven-and-a-half months pregnant, when it was decided to abort the foetus she was carrying. A saline solution was injected into her womb, which doctors thought would kill the foetus within hours.

Incredibly, the procedure failed, and Gianna was born alive thanks, in part, to an astounded, quick-thinking nurse. She was so taken aback by Gianna's live delivery that she summoned an ambulance to whisk her from the abortion clinic to the hospital. Gianna weighed only two pounds at birth and had to stay in hospital for almost three months.

In an ironic twist of fate, the abortionist had to sign her birth certificate.

Gianna is now left with cerebral palsy, as a direct result of the procedure carried out on her in the womb. But after being mercilessly burned alive for 18 hours Gianna was delivered alive. Remarkably, it states on her birth records that she was born after a saline abortion.

Because of her cerebral palsy her foster mother was told that Gianna was unlikely to ever crawl or walk, but courageously battling against the odds, Gianna eventually learned to sit, crawl, and then stand.

She started to walk with leg braces, and by the age of four was walking with the aid of a walker and is now walking without assistance.

Does she blame her mother for leaving her with this condition? Gianna says: "I've never been angry with her because she's a stranger. She hasn't said she's sorry and I know that she had another abortion after me."

"But I don't feel sad or bitter because we can choose to overcome and be sweet or we can overcome and be angry. I want to be the former," She adds with calm firmness.

Gianna Jessen speaks from the heart of Christ as a committed Christian when she concludes: "At this point, I don't want to be in touch with my biological mother. But it's not that I'm angry with her – I forgive her totally".

Life and death are closely related, and so are the arguments that go with them. One of the fundamental and basic objections supporting anti-abortion is the argument sometimes put forward against capital punishment: What right do humans have to curtail the life, or potential life, of something that God has created in His image?

Children are both the parents' and this planet's gift from God.

The abortion experience itself is very traumatic for a woman to endure and no one should underestimate the shame and isolation they may encounter in later years.

Women's experiences of an abortion vary – for some, it may have been a decision made at a vulnerable young age and later regret while for others, it may have involved some level of coercion, or a decision made after the trauma of rape.

But regardless of the circumstances, inner healing is possible if they are willing to accept God's love and grace. Even the most soul-breaking experiences imaginable can be used as the foundation for building a richer, deeper, and more meaningful life.

Over the last few years, we have repeatedly witnessed the push that is on to legalise some forms of euthanasia through parliament. Several years ago, the debate on the value of embryonic human life was highlighted by the stem cell research issue and whether such research could – in addition to working with adult stem cells – also work with cells from embryos with their consequent destruction. This in turn has re-ignited the debate on when life really begins and how we place a value on human life at any point.

Will the recent disclosure that under new legislation private clinics will be able to advertise abortion services on television and radio challenge us to reconsider the consequence of what it means to be someone made in God's image?

How we view the beginning of life, the quality of life, the value of life is critical to our thinking with respect to abortion, embryo research, cloning, eugenics and euthanasia.

Do we even have reason to believe that what we are facing in the carnal intrusion of life and death is more menacing than any other injustice we have ever witnessed on this planet?

Is Anyone Really Normal?

In his book *Everybody's Normal Till You Get to Know Them* John Ortberg writes: "When we enter relationships with the illusion that people are normal, we resist the truth that they are not. We enter an endless attempt to fix them, control them, or pretend that they are what they're not".

The premise of Ortberg's thinking is that nobody is really normal; we all have quirks, defects and faults that make us very much in need of grace and mercy from God and from others. Likewise, we need to give grace and mercy to others and accept that all people come as they are, rather than expect them to be perfect.

The more we look around and the more we observe, the more it becomes reassuring (at least for me!) to realise that normal may be impossible to define, and what is normal to one person is most definitely not normal to another.

One of the great marks of maturity is to accept the fact that we should take people as they come. The need for community is woven into the very fabric of our being. Nothing else can substitute for the life-giving benefits of connecting with others.

I once heard Don Williams, founding pastor of the Coast Vineyard Christian Fellowship in California, remark that he had read a survey where it stated that 96% of us were brought up in dysfunctional families, a figure that, he argued, was 4% inaccurate!

There are countless ways of living our lives, in an effort to avoid facing our dark side and to conceal our real self, such as becoming a workaholic or even a pious, religious person. Similarly, we can hide behind chemical dependency, materialism, intellectualism, legalism, patronising sweetness, or a controlling nature.

Thankfully, God reveals the benefits of authenticity – what it means to live with an "unveiled face", as the Bible puts it. He encourages us to swap the stones, that are so easy to throw at others, for acceptance. He opens our eyes and heart to empathy and the art of interpreting people justly. He lovingly guides us through the mountains and valleys of conflict, forgiveness, confrontation, exclusion, and gratitude.

"Caring for myself is not self-indulgence," wrote Audre Lorde in her 1988 book *A Burst of Light*, which was written soon after she was diagnosed with cancer for a second time, "It is self-preservation."

Self-care appears to be a sensationalised trend in today's culture, propelled on social media illustrated with photos at the gym, cool selfies, and fancy coffees with hashtags like: #selfcare or #selflove. On the other hand, we Christians can go to the opposite extreme. Sometimes, we are so afraid of looking selfish or self-centred that we neglect ourselves entirely. We can even be deluded into thinking that self-care = narcissism and wear constant exhaustion like a badge of honour.

No, self-care is not an indulgence – self-care is a discipline that often requires mental and spiritual toughness, a deep and personal understanding of our priorities, and a deep respect for both ourselves, and for the people we choose to spend our life with. Self-care is, for example, declining the fourth drink at the works'

Christmas party – or it might even be declining the first drink. It could be refusing to be manipulated or taken for granted – even though we know standing firm will be greeted with an angry response – or turning down extra hours of overtime because we know rest is more important than an impressive bank balance.

A basic tenet of the Christian worldview is that we are to care for others. To care is to provide what is necessary for the health, welfare, maintenance, and protection of someone or something. From the very beginning, we humans were charged with caring for God's creation and everything in it. We have a special responsibility towards our fellow humans, but we also have the responsibility to care for ourselves.

As Ernest Hemingway wrote in *Men Without Women*: "The most painful thing is losing ourselves in the process of loving someone too much and forgetting that you are special too".

We rightly see care as essential to family and social relationships. Bound up within the second great commandment "Love your neighbour as yourself" is the duty of care. But sometimes we can be so preoccupied by being someone else's anchor that we can end up drowning.

I'd love to say that I've arrived at a completely healthy place of self-care, but the truth is, I'm still in the middle of the sobering reality of repentance and renewal. I can say for sure, though, that any freedom in this area hasn't come from just tweaking some habits or having a tougher season of life where consistent self-care is more realistic.

Forgiveness and Reconciliation – The Power of the Cross

You have probably never heard of Joe Aviva or Amy Wall. Neither have I.

Let me share their story:

Several years ago, Joe Avila found himself reading a sign close to where he lives that says: "Please do not drink and drive".

There's a smaller sign underneath that reads: "In honour of Amy Wall".

Joe explains: "Young Amy Wall was a young teenage girl that I killed in 1992 while driving drunk on an American freeway".

It's a stunning statement, but Joe calmly relates how that horrific night brought an end to his life of alcoholism and addiction, yet it took the life of a teenage girl.

After the accident, Joe fled the scene. He does not remember that night, but he remembers what came afterwards: He was charged for second-degree murder at the local Jail. In the days that followed, he was overcome by what he had done. "I was just looking for a way to kill myself," he says, "I was afraid, I was angry, [and] I was sad."

Two lives were destroyed the night Joe Avila killed Amy Wall, but God wouldn't let their story end there.

While preparing for his murder trial, Joe checked into a six-month sobriety programme with the Salvation Army. It was there that, as Joe explains, "God put some people in my life who made me understand what reconciliation was and forgiveness was".

A few months into the programme, Joe came to a decision that would impact him, his family, and the Wall family, too: Just before Easter 1993, he entered the courthouse and changed his plea to "guilty".

Although Joe expressed remorse and went to rehab, the judge still had little faith that Joe was saved from his alcoholism. "I'm sentencing you to

maximum time in prison, which is 12 years," the judge ruled, "and I just hope that you will change".

For the next seven and a half years, Joe was locked up in a jail in California.

Choosing to make the most of his life behind bars, Joe spent his time serving the prison's hospice patients.

Through Prison Fellowship, Joe was able to remain a presence in his daughters' lives, creating a bond no prison bars could separate. He also served in the chapel, sharing the Gospel with his fellow prisoners – the highlight of his incarceration.

On Jan. 6, 1999, Joe Avila was released and went home to his family and friends. Thankfully, New Hope Community Church was ready to welcome Joe and his family with open arms. "The pastor had been preparing the congregation for my return for several months," Joe says. Oak trees surrounded the church. "Every one of those trees had a yellow ribbon around it," Joe recalls. "And there was a big banner at the entrance of the church that said, 'Welcome Home, Joe.'"

When Joe saw this, he knew that New Hope would become his home Church, and he's been going there ever since.

Not long after Joe's release, his mentor called to say that

Amy's brother, Derek, wanted to meet with him. For years, Joe had prayed that God would help him reconcile with Amy's family. Even so, Joe was naturally nervous about the meeting.

That first meeting with Derek was several hours long.

Derek told Joe about all the things he and Amy used to do together, how much he loved his sister, and that he had viewed Joe as a monster who should get the electric chair for what he had done.

But then Derek explained that his family had been following Joe's progress behind bars. They knew he was trying to make his life better. Joe told Derek something he had long wanted to say: "I'm really sorry for what I've done, and I hope that someday you can forgive me".

Later, Joe's mentor called again. This time, Rick Wall, Amy's father wanted to see Joe. During that meeting, something miraculous occurred.

Rick told Joe about the two days a year when he visits Amy's grave – on her birthday and the anniversary of her death. And then Rick said, "Joe, I know what you've been doing for a long time now, even when you were in prison, and I approve of it."

Joe's prayers for reconciliation were being answered. "Rick Wall, Amy's father, forgave me before I even asked him to forgive me," Joe says.

He next met with Amy's mum, who insisted he watch a three-hour video of Amy's life before their meeting. "I really got to know Amy that night," said Joe, "and how precious she was and what a tragedy happened when I took her life."

Joe admits it was painful to seek forgiveness from the Walls, but he knew God could use the situation for His glory if he did. His relationship with the Wall family continued to grow, and both Joe and Derek were asked to participate in a Restorative Justice Council event in front of hundreds of people.

The night of the event, Amy's father approached Joe, hugged him, and said, "I love you, Joe".

Years later, Rick's actions and words that evening still deeply affect Joe.

"I killed his daughter," he says, his voice quivering with emotion, "and he was able to give me a hug and say, 'I love you.'"

And that is a true testament to the miracle of reconciliation and why Christ did die on the cross."

Good Friday – Not Bad or Sad Friday

As we approach Good Friday, many minds will be elsewhere. Is this due to an indifference resting on misunderstanding? Someone being raised from the dead? In this sophisticated age, when myth has made way for science, how could anybody take such a claim seriously? Well, that's what I condescendingly thought for many years.

But perhaps it would have been appropriate for me to lay aside any dogmatic scepticism and cynicism which asserts "It's highly improbable" and been brave enough to examine whether, according to the widespread evidence available and the emptiness in my own heart, the resurrection of Christ really did occur as foretold by the Prophets. After all, it was not mere man who raised Christ – it was the Creator of the Universe.

Sadly, cynicism is a regrettable characteristic in human nature, especially in macho Scotland. We might be willing to sing *The Old Rugged Cross* at a Karaoke in Benidorm or sing it with great gusto walking home blootered from the pub. When we witness something noble and beautiful, for a while we tolerate it, even admire it, then we feel the need to pull it down.

Such a pinnacle of goodness is Jesus Christ. It is also the case regarding our film and sports stars – for as long as they exceed our expectations we idolise them, but as soon as they show any sign of fallibility, we pull them down.

Time, distance, and culture separate us from the brief period Jesus walked the earth. Our present-day encounters with Christ come through modern lenses and filters that can distort our view of Him. Even some people in Church seem hellbent on stripping Him of His divinity, making Him out to be no more than a moral teacher.

The genius and paradox of Jesus' ministry is: He reveals that God uses tragedy, suffering, and pain to bring us closer to Him. So, there are no dead ends. There is always hope. After all, on the cross, God took the worst thing – the slaying of Himself – and made it into the best thing: The redemption of the world.

The truth is: We are the ones who must die to self. Authentic faith may a

ways be largely about us, but not in an arrogant or an egotistical way. It's saying: You change first, before you can be an example to someone else.

If we gaze upon the mystery of the cross long enough, we'll eventually view things as being neither totally good nor totally bad. That is why Friday before Easter is called Good Friday. Only at the cross we can learn humility, patience, compassion, and all the Fruits of the spirit that can help us to help others. In effect, the Resurrection turns the tables in an incredible paradigm shift.

No longer are we doing something for God; He, in Jesus Christ, is doing something for us.

No longer are we drawn by our needs to God; He, through Jesus Christ, is drawn by His compassion for us.

Easter – Time to Let Go of the Pain of the Past

Let Easter weekend be the time we refuse to be haunted by the ghosts of the past, embittered by the pain of perceived injustice or betrayal. After all, this weekend we celebrate the ultimate victory over injustice and betrayal.

Holding a grudge and harbouring anger and resentment are simply poison to the soul. We know this, but we still let people get under our skin. It's okay to get even with people, but not with those who hurt us. Ignore them, for God will take care of them. Even though those who betray us as are part of a greater plan, Jesus couldn't get to the cross without Judas' betrayal.

Ultimately, the best revenge is to respond in a totally different manner to the one who caused the offence and the hurt. Instead, get even in the manner of those who have helped and supported us in our times of need – match their compassion, grace, and commitment.

We don't need to be anyone's pushover, or cow tow to the unreasonable demands of others, but we are called by the One who sacrificed His life for us all to rise above the circumstances in which we live.

Don't attempt to get ahead of anybody, for in doing so we won't find true peace and contentedness. In truth, bitterness and peace can never co-exist in our hearts.

Let's continually aim to be the best we can possibly be within our own skin – that will always be good enough for the God of grace and forgiveness.

CHRISTMAS IS STILL MAGICAL

Christmas is a magical time for a child. I loved Christmas as a bairn, as it was all about receiving. The smells of Christmas in adulthood remind me of the smells of my childhood and, as a kid, the most glorious mess in the world was the mess created in the living room on Christmas Day.

I always hoped my mother wouldn't clean it up too quickly – I craved to keep the Christmas magic going for as long as possible!

We know that Christmas is a time of rejoicing and being merry, but it doesn't always work out that way for us, does it? It certainly can be difficult to accept some of the stressful and sorrowful twists and turns that life brings our way. We are trying to cope with our own personal challenges but also dealing with the ever-increasing fuel prices, astronomical bills, and the ongoing threat of the Russia – Ukraine conflict.

Many can be looking forward to Christmas without a care in the world, but others may be looking towards the celebration of our Saviour's birth with sadness, worry, even dread, or trepidation. I know people who are praying that they'll just make it through Christmas – not anticipating anything good will come from a gathering with extended family and friends.

Sadness is real. Worry is real. Anxiety is real.

We stress over our wayward teenage son or daughter, potential debt problems we are facing, worry about our alcohol dependant husband or father, having to face our first Christmas without someone we dearly loved, or celebrating the miracle birth while coming to terms with a critical illness.

It is possible to be surrounded by people and still feel lonely and isolated.

Loneliness is never the product of heaven. Among our Eternal Father's first recorded words were these: "It is not good for man to be alone". (Genesis 2:18).

The last two years have left many of us lonelier than ever, but God's cure for the lonely heart at Christmas is not found in a bottle or wrapped up in a present – It lies in a manger: The Babe of Bethlehem.

Even at its corniest, Christmas touches the hardest of hearts. Who can remain unmoved by hearing children sing *Away in a manger*? The simple story of eternal love in the form of the infant Christ reaches the places other stories don't reach.

If we didn't have the magic of Christmas, would life be the same, especially for children?

We desperately need Christmas because it shines a radiant light for us in this northern hemisphere, piercing a dark and gloomy winter.

The Christmas story continues to entice us, despite secularisation.

That is the reason why we gather in Church on Christmas Eve: Searching and yearning, with alcohol breath and with hope in our hearts, ready to hear the same old story of Jesus and His birth.

Do We Have Room for Jesus in Our Hearts?

I spent so much of my life treating Christmas simply as a great time for excess eating or a time for houses and towns to be lit up like Blackpool illuminations. I was, therefore, oblivious to God's eternal plan for our salvation and redemption – a perfectly synchronized programme of events centred around our Saviour's birth in Bethlehem.

Luke is the only writer in the Bible to use the word "manger" in the New Testament. And what he does with this one word, what God does with this feeding trough, is enough to make us leap for joy.

Manger comes from the Latin word for chew or eat. It refers to a trough where horses, donkeys and cattle eat – a dire place for the God Incarnate to be born.

The apostle Paul tells us: "When the fullness of the time came, God sent forth His Son, born of a woman, born under the Law, so that He might redeem those who were under the Law, that we might receive the adoption as sons". (Galatians 4:4-5)

The inn we read about was a million miles from being a five-star hotel. It was not a place you would want to take your family to on holiday or impress a girlfriend with on a date. It was merely a farm animals' enclosure. Apparently, some of these inns had apartments for travellers, but there was no food, no reception at the entrance and no night porter.

There was no room, even in the poorest of places where animals were kept. No kettle with tea and biscuits in the stable; all the innkeeper provided was hay for the animals and a fire for food preparation and warmth.

The town of Bethlehem was crowded because of the census, and there was no room for Mary and Joseph. The innkeeper was not cruel or inhospitable; he simply didn't have any room left and the poor couple had no relatives in the capital city.

As far as we can determine, they were all alone and completely dependent upon God to provide for all their needs. On reflection, we can think that Mary and Joseph would have said that God provided all they needed.

"No room in the inn" became prophetic words of the truth: "He came unto His own and His own received Him not". (John 1:11)

And the question for us all tonight is: Is there room in my heart for Jesus?

There are hearts in this nation that will never welcome Jesus, not because of hatred towards Him, but simply because their hearts are already overcrowded with thoughts of personal satisfaction and achievement, of worldly success, pleasure, business affairs, etc.

They may say His name in vain, like a swear word – not out of malice – but there is no love, respect, or thanks either. Even as Christians we can at times be half-hearted, lukewarm, and apathetic, like the Church in Loadicia. It's often difficult to prioritise Jesus in our fast-paced lives. "Maybe some other day I will really commit myself to following Jesus," we might say, "but just not today".

What is our attitude towards Jesus? Is He, to us, also a casual swearword? Is He someone we sing about on Sundays in Church, or at Christmas and Easter, to subsequently forget about Him for the rest of the year? Or is He our Lord and Saviour?

Some of the saddest words are: "We don't have room for you" and Jesus knew the sound of those words. He was still in His mother Mary's womb when the innkeeper said, "We don't have room for you". And when He hung on the cross, wasn't the message one of utter rejection? "We don't have room for you in this world".

Today, Jesus is given the same treatment – He goes from heart to heart, asking if He might enter.

Every so often, though, He is welcomed; someone throws open the door of his or her heart and invites Him to stay. And to that person Jesus gives His great promise. If you are still seeking and searching, remember we are all promised: "In my Father's house are many rooms". (John 14:2)

So, there is enough room for you.

My prayer at Christmas is that you make room for Him in your heart, just like Jesus makes room for you in His house!

Each of us is an innkeeper who decides whether there is room for Jesus or not.

The Power of Prayer
at Christmas

Christmas always seemed to be a challenging time for me. I twice experienced a painful separation in a relationship around Christmas time and when I wasn't in a relationship, it was the only time of year that I struggled with being on my own.

I would quite often leave my hometown of Portsoy to celebrate Christmas elsewhere. I remember going to visit family in Blyth, Northumberland, travelling to Inverness several times, and a Christmas spent in Aviemore.

These became times of much prayer, and I welcomed the release from the pressures and humdrum of business and local Church.

Be it in silence or out loud, we can pray anytime by ourselves, in a small group or together with an entire congregation. To pray, we don't have to be a pastor or a particularly clever or religious person, nor do we have to be going through a hard time or have the perfect life; all we need is to have a simple faith and the willingness to seek God.

What should I pray for, you might ask? Well, how about we pray for others less fortunate than we are, or for someone's peace or healing?

As I type this blog/devotional, I very much have three local people in my heart for prayer – two members of the same family who have been diagnosed with Huntington's Disease in their 30s, and someone else I know who has recently been diagnosed with MS.

Don't neglect the power of prayer at Christmas. Prayer is the window that God has placed within the four walls of our world. Leave it shut, and the world is a cold, dark, and isolated house, but throw back the curtains and let in His light and open the window to hear His voice.

Let us open the window of prayer and invoke the presence of God in our life.

Don't we need some "Peace on Earth and Goodwill to all Mankind"?

Don't we need some "Silent Night, Holy Night"?

Don't we need the appearance of angels, the sudden joy of shepherds and the blessed hope of a Baby whose very name means 'God within us'?

Reminiscing on the Daft Days Following Christmas

Somewhere between December 27th and December 31st, time becomes quite abstract – a type of "no man's land" – and it can be hard to know what to do with ourselves, although the bairns might be in their element watching the snow fall as they look out of the window! But in the aftermath of the festive season, we're left to navigate post-Christmas life holding a tin of Quality Street with only the sweeties that no one likes lying at the bottom.

Christmas time is technically not over but it feels like it is. We've stuffed ourselves with turkey, cranberry jelly, roast tatties, and Brussels sprouts. We have maybe overindulged with the traditional refreshments, and we've unwrapped every present under the tree.

As a young lad, Boxing Day was always great fun for me, as it was a chance to get stuck into the *Broons* or the *Oor Wullie* annuals or, in later years when my football fanaticism grew stronger, my *Shoot* or *Topical Times* annuals.

Games were a great novelty for a week or two, before they were dumped in the back of the press again, with Connect Four, Monopoly and Spirograph three of the most popular.

It was time to settle down and watch all the Christmas repeats on our TV with only three channels of which just two of them were watchable – BBC2 usually tried to pretend it wasn't Christmas!

Scotland has its history – a very proud one, I may add. When you have history, you also have traditions, and Scotland has traditions stretching back hundreds of years. What we proud Scots love more than tradition is food. And what we love more than food is drink – and loads of it!

When we expertly blend tradition, food, and drink together, we have the perfect recipe to create a custom that has lasted centuries and has no sign of letting up.

What many of us don't realise is that Christmas in Scotland was banned for nearly 400 years. Apparently, in 1583, the Glasgow Kirk at St Mungo's Cathedral – now Glasgow Cathedral – ordered the seemingly excessive excommunication of those who celebrated Yule, while elsewhere in Scotland, even singing a Christmas carol was considered a serious crime. In fact, it was The Scottish Presbyterian Church led by its founder, John Knox, that decided to cancel the festive season, forbidding any Christmas holiday festivities. What a party pooper the great reformer was!

Any activity that was judged to be extravagant, or celebrated superstitions, was deemed un-Christian and therefore banned. The 12 days between Christmas and Twelfth Night were given over to getting merry with the period hailed as the "daft days" by esteemed 17th-century Scots poet Robert Fergusson.

And that's how things were until the Victorian era, which saw a revival in festive celebrations when Prince Albert brought many rituals back from Germany, which form the Christmas we recognise today.

By the 1800s, people had become more relaxed about observing Christmas, but it meant that Hogmanay, or the turning of the New Year, was the true festive celebration, although it wasn't until the late 1950s that Christmas Day and Boxing Day finally became recognised holidays for us Scots.

Christmas can also be a time of reminiscing, and this came up in my FB memories where I had spent Christmas in Inverness for the third time in four years – three months before my MND diagnosis:

"Today, Boxing day, just having returned from Church, the same sense of thankfulness is still there in my heart, pounding away. I waddled back along the banks of River Ness struggling to get my left leg to work as freely as my right! But this simple revelation came to mind: Not only are we still alive but we are all loved by the same Lord who first loved us".

Things in my life, and probably your life too, may not be as I would choose right now if I'm honest. But let's all of us who believe in the Christian God of the Bible, and even those who struggle or refuse to, be grateful that we are still drawing breath, experiencing care and compassion for those who sit at the Christmas dinner table alone or with an empty chair or two.

And let us, as the old hymn reminds us, count our blessings one by one.

Let's Value What Really Matters

When we are in the final days of our lives, what will we want or crave most? Will we hug that University degree in the expense frame that hangs on the wall? Will we ask to be carried to the garage, so we can sit in our precious car? Will we find comfort in rereading our financial statements online? Will we regret not making that extra investment when we had the cash? Or will we be clinging onto sexual conquests, business success or famous fitba mementos?

What will matter, then, will be the people we value and love; those who were always with us in our darkest and loneliest times. If relationships will matter most then, shouldn't they matter most now? When dealing with people, it's easy to forget that we are not dealing with creatures of logic but with creatures of emotion, and we all fall into that category. Our relationships are our bedrock, our foundation. We need to nurture them with the love, grace, and attention they deserve.

Ultimately, we are wasting our life if we neglect what we were designed to do. And every human being created in the image of God was designed to reflect the glory of God, the worth of God, the beauty of God. So, if we don't find our joy in Christ, if we don't find our satisfaction in Christ but, instead, find it in other things that may in the short run look satisfying, we have wasted our lives.

That is not only the tragedy of our own lives but also a great dishonour to God, and we will find, at the end of our lives, that we have wasted that life, if we have treated God as marginal instead of central.

It's so easy for us to take those nearest to us for granted, or to drive ourselves insane by pursuing what is clearly futile or unattainable. Let's not prioritise the wrong things or pander to the wrong people, because, as we all know, life on earth is short. Look back ten years and it seems like only yesterday.

Never let us be afraid to reset our priorities and start over again. It can often be daunting after a major disappointment, and we may have learned some painful lessons, but we are not starting from scratch – we are starting from a place of valuable experience.

The hands of time wait for no one, let's prioritise the things and people that really matter. Let's somehow muster up the strength to face each day, however bad we feel, with a grateful heart thanking our Father in Heaven for the things and people who really matter.

Life Matters.